THE BEST AUSTRALIAN HUMOROUS WRITING

THE BEST AUSTRALIAN HUMOROUS WRITING

EDITED BY ANDREW O'KEEFE + STEVE VIZARD

MELBOURNE
UNIVERSITY
PRESS

MELBOURNE UNIVERSITY PRESS
An imprint of Melbourne University Publishing Limited
187 Grattan Street, Carlton, Victoria 3053, Australia
mup-info@unimelb.edu.au
www.mup.com.au

In association with x15 PTY LTD

First published 2008
Introduction © x15 PTY LTD, 2008
Text © for all articles remains with individual authors
Collection © x15 PTY LTD, 2008
Design and typography © Melbourne University Publishing Limited, 2008

Every attempt has been made to locate the copyright holders for material
quoted in this book. Any person or organisation that may have been
overlooked or misattributed may contact the publisher.

Designed by Alice Graphics
Typeset by J & M Typesetting
Printed in Australia by Griffin Press

National Library of Australia Cataloguing-in-Publication entry:

The best Australian humorous writing / editors Andrew O'Keefe, Steve Vizard.

9780522855944 (pbk.)
Australian wit and humour—Collections.
O'Keefe, Andrew
Vizard, Steve.

A827.08

Contents

Politics

Society

Environment, Science and Technology

Popular Entertainment

The Arts

Introduction

When I was nine, my brother Andy and I cut out a mail-order advertisement from the back page of our *Phantom* comic. The small advertisement promised delivery within seven days of "the world's best collection of postage stamps sourced from all four corners of the globe". I remember the word "best", just as I remember the expression "all four corners of the globe".

Andy watched as I reverentially filled out the form and then we walked hand in hand to the post box at the end of Inverness Way, beyond which the known world ended.

These were the hazy days when summers came earlier and were hotter and drier and bluer. For seven days Andy and I sweated by our letterbox as cicadas roared and Mrs Pappas and the other neighbours smiled in collusion. On the seventh day, exactly as promised, the postie's whistle sounded.

It was a tiny brown cardboard box, the sort we had read about in Enid Blyton stories, the sort that never arrive now. I removed the lid and paper sprang out like square confetti.

The world's best stamps.

Andy and I painstakingly set them out in rows on the good dining room table. One hundred and thirty-seven stamps in all. Five

Australian kangaroos. Exotic triangular stamps marked Polska and Yemen featuring animals. I remember a leopard and a monster butterfly with luminescent blue wings. A dull stamp with pictures of a city by a lake from somewhere called Helvetia. And one grey stamp featuring a profile that even a nine year old couldn't fail to identify, the visage of Adolf Hitler.

And I remember thinking, the best? The best? How can I know this is the best?

There was no doubt that the 137 stamps were good. To a highly trained 9-year-old's eye it was patently clear the Hitler stamp alone must be a scarce collector's item. Andy and I were fairly confident after deliberation that the Führer must have personally licked our stamp, most probably in his bunker or at the 1936 Olympic Games, and we dreamt of Messerschmitts and Jesse Owens.

But the best?

Surely there were other stamps that might have qualified for the best. We didn't know much about philately but we knew enough to recall a zeppelin stamp, an upside-down zeppelin, which had failed to find its way into our box. And wasn't there something about a Penny Black that might have made the cut?

Why had they called it the best? Who had picked the best? Was it a man? Or a woman? What did they look like? Did they have children like me? Where had they made their decisions? Was it in a room? I remember the location printed on the cardboard box was a mysterious Hornsby. Who were these Hornsby arbiters of all that is best? Was there a committee? A discussion? A vote? What did their kids say? Come to think of it, surely the Hornsby experts hadn't gone through this whole process of advertising on the back of *Phantom* and selecting the cream of the crop merely to dispatch one box of stamps? Were there other boxes of the best nestled in other canvas postie sacks in the other back streets of our continent?

Were their bests the same as our best? How many types of best are there?

I struggled to sleep each night in the countdown to the arrival of Father Christmas, certain these questions would plague me forever. Or until the arrival three weeks later of a red 26" Malvern Star, the best two-wheeler ever made.

After that long summer our lives were forever calibrated by a succession of bests.

The best showbag at the Royal Agricultural Show, a mouth-watering assortment of Bertie Beetles and chocolate frogs and cartoons, purchased as we twelve year olds trudged past sheds of bloated Herefords and arenas of axe-yielding Tasmanian timbermen, pondering how to maximise our 20-cent investment.

The best dozen Australian wine assortment, a mix of Australia's best reds and best whites as offered by Westpac in an envelope containing my monthly bank statements.

The best of the seventies, a musical compilation of original recordings, a late-night television offer: phone now and we'll toss in the best of the nineties.

The best university, the best cricketer, the best school, the best airline, the best of ABBA, the best of the best.

If the best is mercurial, the best humorous writing is totally elusive. One publisher contacted for clearance rights to an essay for inclusion in this anthology remarked of our request, "If it's supposed to be humorous, why would you want to include a piece by him? He writes about politics". Spitting out the word politics, as though the subject were the black hole of humour. Conflating object and form. Forgetting that humour is rarely about what one is looking at, but almost always how.

It is true, some subjects are more intrinsically amusing than others. Sir Ian McKellen as Lear disrobing to reveal his mesmerisingly outsize member gives Germaine Greer a head start. And Rude

Food, the subject of Graeme Blundell's television critique, raises a smirk before a word is read.

Even if the subjects are not intrinsically funny, all of the writers represented in this collection are. Humour more than any other human condition is in the eye of the beholder. Each of these writers has a knack of beholding things through funny eyes.

In choosing works for this volume we have tried to accommodate the fickleness of subjectivity and have cast our net wide. Represented here is a large number of creators writing in a variety of styles across many media.

There is a diversity of form—essays, reviews, commentary, opinions, editorials and even poetry, such as Les Murray's distilled reflections on fame.

There is a diversity of subject matter. From Julia Zemiro's reminiscences of shoplifting and her childhood relationship with her father, to Clive James's personal encounter with climate change.

For most of 2007 the nation's attention was devoted to the prospect of an Australian federal election. Several of the works take the inexorable manoeuvrings towards November as their subject, including Mungo MacCallum's commentary on the doomed Coalition campaign; Kaz Cooke's reflections on Julia Gillard and the public's expectations of female politicians; Guy Rundle's reversioning of *The West Wing*; and Frank Devine's opinions on political schadenfreude.

Unlike essayists, writers of humour often set their sights low, microscopically low, targeting the minutiae of everyday life. For Catherine Deveny it's the outrage at the owners of 4WDs; for Barry Cohen it's the problem of modern telecommunication providers; and for Wendy Harmer it's the gripe of entertaining children, even her own. Tiny targets and large truths.

The media, television in particular, continue to play a growing role in the lives of all Australians and they have a commensurate significance in many of our contributions, including *The Chaser*'s thoughts about the Logie Awards and Marieke Hardy's reflections on the curvaceous television chef Nigella Lawson.

Surprisingly, Australia lacks a tradition of publications dedicated to humorous writing, such as Britain's *Punch, Private Eye* and *Spectator*, or *National Lampoon* and *The New Yorker* in the United States. In any case, we have sought to include a diversity of original publishers and intended readers—newspapers, quarterly essays, academic journals, magazines, speeches, public broadcasters. And there is a spread of the internationally famous and those who deserve to be much better known.

As to the perennial question—Do Australians have a distinctively Australian sense of humour?—we leave that to the reader. It is true that the editor's job is to make a selection, and it goes without saying that this anthology is representative of what we find humorous. But at its heart, this is a selection intended for those who want to find their own connections. There is no fundamental order. There is no narrative throughline, no implied thesis, nor a beginning, middle and end. On the contrary, there are myriad beginnings, plenty of middles and at least two ends. The connections in this anthology might be found less in the order we have imposed upon the works, more in what the reader finds and how the reader uses them. The connections will be found in random readings on a beach towel, on a toilet or waiting in an airport lounge. It is a lucky dip. It is a lazy Sunday morning yum cha. It is a best value showbag.

Something for everyone might be one way of describing this collection.

Whether the something is enough, or the everyone is too many, is ultimately a matter for each reader. It is true the anthology contains almost fifty pieces, a ridiculous number even by Hits of the Seventies compilation standards. Some will argue less is more. Possibly. But this anthology is designed for those who remember hotter, bluer, sunnier summers and believe more is more.

Many years on, I can say with certainty that the small box of postage stamps was indeed the best collection in the only way that mattered. It was the best to me.

Andrew O'Keefe
and Steve Vizard
September 2008

Everyday Life

OLGA PAVLINOVA OLENICH

Teacherwoman

Perhaps a quarter of a century ago. Can it be that long? A tech school in the northern suburbs of Melbourne. Near the large sprawling cemetery and the big Ford factory. Convenient for the Turkish workers who are dying like flies. Not so convenient for me. I have to come in from the city on the train which smells of piss and beer and cigarettes. I try not to look at my fellow passengers. Eye contact not recommended.

I am very young. Straight out of uni. I've decided to become a teacher because I want to travel and I need the money. Around Christmas I saw an ad in the papers asking for graduates to swell the depleted ranks of the much-maligned profession. The offer is a good one. It is not the conventional route into teaching. There is no contract to go out there and teach in some godforsaken country town for two years; there is just the offer of money and some "training" which turns out to be the biggest hoax since Ern Malley had a go. The lecturers are less qualified than I am and more interested in getting me into the sack than imparting any skills or knowledge of the "how to be a teacher" kind. Not that you can teach anyone to be a teacher. As I am about to find out. Of course, I have volunteered for the least palatable of the schools on offer. I figure, if I'm going to do this, I'm going to do it without the sugar coating. No *Prime of Miss Jean Brodie* for me.

Roger Hale is sitting in the rubbish bin again. He is a squirt of a kid with a nasty intelligent little face. The intelligence is a surprise but not a good one. He gets away with murder in a place where intelligence goes unrecognised. I leave him in the rubbish bin. From the first English lesson, I have realised that making a fuss about it is just what he expects and hopes for. He is prepared for the standoff. Past experience has taught him he will win. He is a lot more clever than the average teacher and he knows it. He starts classes by sitting in the rubbish bin and shocking his teacher. This is how he provokes the first joust and how he gets control. So he was outraged when I ignored him the first time and let him spend the whole hour in the bin, which must have been uncomfortable. Now it's a matter of principle for him to sit in the bin throughout my English class.

English! Now there's a subject you want to be teaching in a flimsy portable classroom stuck out on a dry paddock away from the main buildings like some stinking outhouse, especially to a class of boys, described on the tatty cover of their class roll as "3F–K". 3F–K. What brilliant bureaucratic mind decided that the dead-end class of adolescent boys who were just waiting to get out of school at the magic age of fifteen should be categorised as 3F–K? Were there no other cut-off points in the alphabet that might have served just as well? Of course, some of the boys have got to the roll already. The cover is very decorative. The word *fuck* appears forty-two times, mostly spelt correctly but with the occasional aberration, a "c" left out, an "o" where the "u" should be. ESL I presume, or perhaps not. Everything is possible in 3F–K. And then there are the illustrations. Crude is an inadequate word to describe what has been drawn on the cover of the 3F–K roll. Anyway, it's a start, I tell them, waving the thing in front of me. It's a poem. An illustrated poem. It rhymes. What does it rhyme with, apart from itself: fuck, fuck, fuck?

"Stuck," says Roger from the bin and I start laughing. So do the 3F–K boys. Even Roger can't help laughing. He makes a show of struggling out of the bin.

"Fuck miss, I'm stuck," he says. It's hilarious. We are screaming with laughter. I sober up eventually and take up the posture of the schoolteacher again. It strikes me, for the first time, that it's lucky I'm in a portable where no-one can hear us. It also strikes me that I was born to this teaching thing. A frightening thought, but the adrenalin is pumping. I'm actually loving this. And I can smell victory. Blow me away if I haven't got to these boys. They're laughing: they're looking at me with anticipation, and laughing. I've actually got to them. It's going to be some struggle but I just know that I've got to them. In an instant, I know.

The Turks are okay. They've still got a residual respect for the institution of school, not quite the veneration they would have had for the village school back in Turkey, but something of the old attitudes remains, something their parents have managed to drill into them between the crippling shifts at the Ford factory. The teacher is the teacher. An important person. Well, maybe. The Yugoslavs are a different matter. They're just plain insolent. I'm young. I'm a "girl" with a Russian name, not so foreign to their ears, and there is no way they're going to let me boss them around. Three of them are called Dragan. I find this quite amusing. So amusing that I invent an excuse to call them over the PA system under the eye of the very conventional principal who doesn't suspect me until I make the announcement. "Would all the dragons in 3F–K come to the music room to practise their scales," I say glibly, and I give the principal a sweet look. He is clearly confused. Not so the Dragans who may be thick but have never been called up like this before and see it as a kind of honour. The staff are laughing. The Dragans are laughing.

"Gotcha!" I think.

It's not all as sweet as that, however. One of the Turks is accused of raping a girl in 3A–E. We never see the girl again. She is removed to a Catholic school where it is presumed she will be safe and I meet a policeman who warns me about the boy.

"Now listen, luv," he says, "don't you worry. We've got him scared. He should be okay in the classroom. Any trouble, let me know."

"Yes, constable," I say and feel as if I'm in a *Carry On* movie. But even though I've grown up in the western suburbs, the daughter of poor reffos, I've had a sheltered life. I've never come across situations like this before. I am both horrified by the boy and understanding, in a strange way. I hope the girl hasn't been raped, but I can never be sure. I waver between crying for her and crying for the boy who comes to school looking like a whipped dog. I'm on a seesaw and I feel sick. Some days I wonder if I can face another day at this school.

I have no choice but to get better. After Easter, I begin to teach art as well as English. This is decided when the art teacher leaves without warning. Something to do with despair, I should imagine, but I am excited by the art room which is astonishingly big and well equipped. I have also become the form-teacher of 3F–K which means I see them first thing every morning and that they come to me when they're in trouble. *When* they're in trouble! I don't often get away from school until well after five, sometimes as late as seven when it is getting dark and the walk to the station becomes a bit of a nightmare. With the requisite tombstones, no less.

The Maltese kid in 3F–K is my star art student. I've worried about him since the first day. He's so obviously effeminate. I wonder that they haven't done him over yet. The delicacy of his hands intrigues me. They are long, and the fingers seem to have no joints, like the fingers of Christ in a Byzantine icon. John helps me to set up the room before classes and we talk. His mother is widowed. Some factory accident, but I don't go into it because I can see how John's already pallid face drains of all colour when he mentions his father. John is fastidious. He arranges the brushes and the poster paints in long rows along the front table, explaining that it will be easier for students to see what they need, especially because he has graded the colours of the paints, put the blues near the greens and the reds near the yellows and the purples near the … it all looks like a cubist painting. Then it looks like a mess. Because the others storm in and grab anything they can lay their hands on, anything they can flick, anything they can poke with, anything they can splash on each other in the course of the lesson. It's chaotic, but amazing things begin to happen in the chaos.

There are some good artists in the class. Valentino Calluzzi is one of them. He is a stocky Italian with eyebrows that meet over his nose like Frida Kahlo's. I tell him this and show him a picture of her with Diego Rivera. Valentino says Diego looks like his Uncle Paolo. I reckon Diego does look like someone's Uncle Paolo and I say that Frida could have had someone more attractive. Valentino says that women often like ugly men. This is the most I've ever heard from Valentino. He is reputed to have a shocking temper and I am instinctively wary of him. With good cause.

In the English class, I have the 3F–K boys working on an obscene magazine that is gradually becoming quite respectable. They've changed the name from *Fuck Off* to *I Gotta Get Outta Here* which I secretly like a lot but I keep telling them it's awful so that they feel they're winning a fight. By this stage, they have a nickname for me. It's Dracula. Not surprising. I have long dark hair and I'm usually dressed in black. Something to do with ballet, I think. All that getting about in a black leotard. Or maybe, as my friends say, I'm just morbid. Just look at my choice of schools. The school near the cemetery, I ask you. Valentino has come up with a piece about racing cars for the magazine. We are sitting together at the back of the room going over it for spelling mistakes. "Ooaah! Sucking up to Drac!" wisecracks Roger who has left the bin for good and now sits at a table he drags out of the front line of tables at the beginning of each class.

Suddenly Valentino is up on his feet. I spring to mine and throw myself between Valentino and Roger. Valentino is swinging a chair over his head. He throws it at Roger. It hits me in the shoulder and the corner of the back clips the side of my forehead. There is blood and confusion. Valentino stands white and shaking. I think the others are going to kill him. I don't know how I do it, but I stay on my feet and calm things down. Wisecracks about blood and Dracula. A macabre song and dance. Anything for peace. When the others are sitting, I look at Valentino who is still standing and I take him by the arm and lead him outside. I don't know what I am going to say to him. I'm angry. I see that he is about to cry.

I take him by the shoulders. He is about my own height so I am looking directly into his eyes. "You are *never*," I whisper hoarsely as the blood comes down my face in a steady trickle, "you are *never* to throw anything again. Never, never, never!" My throat is dry. I feel myself beginning to shake. I let the boy go. I cross the paddock to get to the staffroom. John runs after me.

"Are you okay miss?"

"Go back to the class, John. And don't let anyone touch Valentino."

When I come back to the portable, they are all miraculously quiet, working away at *I Gotta Get Outta Here*. Only a few dare to sneak a look at me. A lot of them are flushed. We get through the class without a word and then they shuffle out of the classroom shame-faced, as if they had all thrown chairs at me. Valentino is at a loss. His eyebrow is a tight line over his red eyes.

"Sorry miss," he manages to whisper, as he stumbles out of the door.

Later in the week I speak to the principal about Valentino. I do not tell him the whole story. I merely ask if the kid can have some help with controlling his temper. "He needs a good belting," says the principal, and that's that.

The staff let off steam in the staffroom. There are no nice cafes, restaurants or pubs nearby. There are a few shops and a fish'n'chip place where you can get a standard ham and tomato sandwich on white bread, maybe with some lettuce and a slice of beetroot thrown in. So you go to the shops and take back your fish'n'chips or your sandwich to the staffroom where there is an enormous metal urn, a big tin of Maxwell House instant coffee and a bowl of tea bags. It's a tech school. Up until recently, the staff was entirely male, and there is still the feeling that women don't belong here. There is a big green snooker table at one end of the long rectangular room. There is smoke. Everyone smokes, except me. Much to the alarm of some of the more hard-bitten tradies, I take up snooker.

There is some resistance, at first. You get the feeling that the wives of these blokes don't do things like play snooker. From what I hear, they don't do much except for domestic duties. They stay at home and give their hubbies a packed lunch to eat in the staffroom. It's only a few of us who have to face the shops. I figure that if I don't do something to bridge the gap between me and the tradies, I won't ever be able to do much for the 3F–K boys in terms of a future except for keeping them moderately entertained during my allotted hours in their awful present. The phalanx of old hands—Les, Kevin, Col and the others whose names I can never remember—is the real powerhouse of the place. This group of men can make or break a kid. They can recommend him for an apprenticeship, they can develop his skills, they can keep him at school and out of the factory for a few more crucial years. I want them on my side, just in case. It's not easy. I'm young. I'm straight from "the university" and I'm also a wog. Three strikes.

It is incredible, but snooker and I obviously have a date with destiny. A bit like the 3F–K boys. Right from the beginning, I find I am a good player. At times, I am a fantastic player. I even show off, rather loudly for a stuck-up university graduate. The blokes stop sniggering and begin to take me seriously. It's a deadly competitive spirit in the staffroom at the snooker table end and a winner is respected. Well, perhaps only a little in my case, but the little bit is just enough for me to be able to ask for some favours for "my boys" when things get a little rough.

Parent–teacher night. The police come to make sure the teachers can move safely from their cars into the building. Ex-students and the older siblings of the currently aggrieved have been known to show up and settle scores. I am dropped off outside the school gates by a friend who cannot believe where I have been going on my working days. "You must be crazy!" he says. I have been to a concert, I am wearing a black velvet suit and my hair is in a plait. I am a little bit nervous, like a ballet dancer about to step out onto the stage.

"Dracula!" One of the Dragans has seen me arrive. The chant goes up. Ten, twenty, fifty voices, at least. And there is the sound of stamping.

"Dracula! Dracula! Dracula!" I hear all around me. I know this is no threat, though the apprehensive looks of some of the staff who are still outside the hall make me realise that they are nervous and not brave enough to confront the mob on my behalf. But I do not need courage, theirs or mine. I have recognised the loud beat of what is really a loving welcome. This chant and the stamping are a kind of applause.

I feel the tears in my eyes. I try to grin but my whole face appears to be quivering, especially my mouth which is jerking wildly at the corners. This is going to be a disaster. Dracula cannot be seen to be crying.

"Are you okay miss?" John is by my side. Under the cover of darkness, he has taken my right hand into his own long smooth one. My heart is ready to burst. I can see it bursting out of my chest— blood gushing everywhere, a fountain of blood where my heart used to be.

"I'm okay. John, I'm fine." But I don't let go of his hand.

WENDY HARMER

Torn between satay skewers and children as an endangered species

Watching my children play over these summer holidays, I've come to the conclusion that the only present Santa should leave under the Christmas tree is other people's children.

Not everyone would agree. The American satirist Fran Lebowitz once observed that "hell is other people's children". But for me, the most hellish six words in the English language are: "Mum, will you play with me?"

(Come on, I know I'm not alone on this one. I'm just brave or rude enough to admit it.)

When other people's children come to play with mine, it's heaven. Then I can get on with things I would rather do—such as scrub the griller tray with steel wool, or poke out my eyes with a satay skewer.

Call me selfish and lazy if you like, but it's the mind-numbing tedium of "imaginative play" which has me screaming for the exits—the interminable sessions of Play Doh, the fiddly craft-making, the excruciating "let's play shops" and dress ups—anything which looks like fun on *Play School*. I figure that's why *Play School* was invented. They have to pay actors to do this stuff with your children. Meanwhile, you can hire other people's children to do the same, at your place, for a cheese toastie and a lime ice-block.

The demographers tell us that the number of families with children is steadily declining in Australian society; that childless, unmarried men and women will soon be the norm, and, if and when they do have children, it will be only one or two.

I had two children late in life and I regret I didn't have four. My children regret it, too. They look at photos of me and my three siblings and love to fantasise about what it would have been like to have two more live-in playmates, just as I look back at photos of my father's seven brothers and sisters and like to imagine.

I can hear the shudders of my generation that grew up with the ideology of zero population growth as a mantra. This idea has been given new life by the present generation of child-bearing age who believe it's not environmentally responsible to have a large family. Or is it the fear that children can be a blunt instrument with the potential to bludgeon to death personal ambitions?

It's all very well for me to look back and fantasise about having a big family. I didn't do it. However, there's a lot to lose when suburbs become dominated by single young men and women living alone in flats. Arid landscapes where children are an endangered species.

A recent family trip to Japan, where the birthrate is one of the world's lowest, revealed a sad reality: playgrounds grown over with weeds and scattered with broken glass; swings and slides rusted and broken. We did not see children anywhere.

Visits to dinky gift-shops sent the owners into a frenzy of anxiety. Children were an unwelcome, unruly intrusion into an ordered, adult, existence. Strangely, there were no children at Tokyo Disney, either. Every ride—from the tea-cup twirly-whirly to the roller coaster—was packed with giggling, infantilised thirty-somethings in Mickey Mouse ears.

Finding an Australian street populated with children is becoming increasingly difficult. Perhaps it's the families, not the elderly, who now need gated communities. A place where parents agree that the sound of children shrieking with laughter is what makes a neighbourhood. We have "wildlife corridors" where possums can meet and form gangs that romp on your roof. So, too, we could have paths where children can meet and have adventures.

Remember when you and the children down the street would roam from dawn till dusk during the summer holidays? Where do children go these days? Judging by the sound coming from the backyard, they're at my place.

While some people place nesting boxes to lure fauna into their backyards, my husband and I have put in a lot of effort to make our yard "kid central". We're lucky to have a big block and a pool. We've strung up the hammock, the rope swings and the trapeze. We scored a trampoline on council clean-up day. Then we added the magic ingredients of ducks and baby chickens. Voila! Tribes of children appeared from every corner of the neighbourhood and our two disappeared.

The Xbox and television have been abandoned. There are any number of commentators who bemoan that children these days suffer from "a lack of imagination". No, what they suffer from is a lack of playmates. And with the best will in the world, a mum who specialises in jigsaw puzzles is a boring substitute.

Observing three little girls spend a day making dollies out of ice-block sticks and pipe cleaners is enough to make a Bratz doll manufacturer blanch. Gangs of smallish boys still stage treasure hunts, sword fights with sticks and build cubby huts out of brooms and bits of corrugated iron. Baby chickens, alas, remain unco-operative circus animals. Some things, thankfully, never change.

So by all means let's make our cities environmentally sustainable, but not at the expense of family size. We need to encourage the next generation to have more children than we do now, and to have them earlier.

Otherwise parents will have to play with their kids—and no one wants to be crawling into a cubby house with 50-year-old knees.

Believe me, I know.

DANNY KATZ

Love is never saying sorry ... so there

You younger readers probably won't know what I'm talking about here—anybody who wasn't around in the 1970s and '80s, that golden era of wonder and joy, when computers were only used for playing Frogger, peanuts hadn't started killing children yet, and circumcised doodles were the cutting-edge of male pret-a-porter high-style fashion. In that glorious age of innocence, there was a famous cartoon series called "Love is ...", which featured a little naked boy and a little naked girl, cuddling and kissing each other, with a romantic caption underneath like "Love is ... being able to say you are sorry" or "Love is ... a picture of happiness", and everyone adored these cartoons because back then, naked eight-year-olds getting it on was considered charming and sentimental. These days you look at cartoons like that, you can wind up doing 14 years in a Cambodian prison with Gary Glitter.

Anyway, because it's Valentine's Day today, I thought it'd be a great opportunity to revive the "Love is ..." cartoon series, but update it for the modern couple of 2008. So here are a few of my ideas for romantic captions—I haven't got round to drawing the pictures yet, but just imagine a naked boy and a naked girl, loosely based on my beloved and me, so she's looking svelte and leggy and cute, and he's looking a bit lank and furry, like something a plumber yanked out of a shower drain at a caravan park in Lorne.

"Love is ... avoiding breaking wind in each other's face." I know it's not always easy, but the message here is, make an effort to leave the room, or at least aim out a doorway. I'm so considerate, I actually go into the backyard, down the side of the house, and stand up against the fence so nobody will be offended or bothered— although Toshio, the Japanese lady next door, does keep calling AGL to report a leak.

"Love is ... tolerating each other's idiotic idiosyncrasies." Sometimes your partner can do things that are a bit grating—and in my beloved's case, it's her grating. She will cook a zucchini dish, and grate nine-tenths of the zucchini into the dish, then put the remaining tenth of the zucchini back in the fridge. WHY COULDN'T SHE JUST USE THAT LAST TENTH? WOULD THE DISH HAVE TASTED SO DIFFERENT WITH A TENTH MORE ZUCCHINI-FLAVOUR? AND NOW WHAT'S ANYONE SUPPOSED TO DO WITH A ZUCCHINI IN THE FRIDGE THAT IS MISSING NINE-TENTHS?

"Love is ... occasionally making like instead of making love." Every couple knows those evenings when you're both feeling schleppy and brain-vegetative and you flomp into bed, then the man makes a half-arsed arse-grab, and the woman gives an enticing flirty "must we?" look, then you both proceed to do something that looks like a couple of 150-year-old giant land tortoises mating in a Galapagos Island documentary.

"Love is ... feigning interest in your partner's stories." Time and time again my beloved will sit and listen to my bi-weekly eight-minute discourse on Kantong's hokkein noodles and how it says "serves four" on the packet but it really only serves three—she'll nod and sigh sympathetically all the way through, even though she's really thinking about Cherry Ripes and the buff black crumper on

So You Think You Can Dance Australia, and how they could maybe be combined.

"Love is ... having conversations that could be a Pinter play." Here's ours from the other day: "Did you say something?/ When I was what?/ When you were talking to her/ What did I say?/ Something you said/ I thought I told you/ Haloumi cheese?" It made total sense when we were saying it.

"Love is ... having a laugh at the expense of others." You can't be stuffed any more with Oscar-Wildean-quippery or topical political-humour. Now, when we need a laugh, we just do cruel impressions of our children after they've gone to bed, or sing Vanessa Amorosi's "Absolutely Everybody" with a white South African accent.

And finally, love is ... always having to say you're sorry.

CATHERINE DEVENY

Listen up, you selfish and ignorant people. Stop driving 4WDs

I would like to sincerely apologise for the comments I made about 4WDs in last week's column.

Due to a limitation on the number of words, I was unable to say everything I wanted about these dangerous and obnoxious monster trucks being driven by people selfish at best and ignorant at worst.

And not just shame on you for driving these anti-social, arrogant four-wheeled bullies. Shame on the car companies for appealing to your insecurity by sucking you in with slogans like "Give way—not" (Jeep), "Get in or get out of the way" (Toyota HiLux) or the "class-kicking" HiLux 4WD utility with its "intimidating styling", "aggressive bonnet scoop" and "dominating moulded front bumpers". YEAH! What next? "Kill everyone and destroy the planet NOW WITH FREE AIR!" Suck up that free air, baby, because soon we'll be paying for it.

When I discovered that the word Pajero really is Spanish for wanker, I thought to myself: "It must be my birthday!"

And just so we are clear, bush folk, people towing horse floats and the like, you're off the hook. I'm talking about the people driving tanks to do the shopping and drop their kids off at school.

I can't be fagged unpacking the arrogance of the space they take up on the road, which is the equivalent of taking up eight seats at the cinema and wearing a refrigerator as a hat. And I'm not going to get into their environmental impact, as there must be at least one 4WD that is greener than the lowered Commodores with mags that fang down my street blowing blue smoke. But you'd have to be an idiot not to put together the basic larger-vehicle-equals-more-fuel-necessary-particularly-on-city-roads equation.

Need the space? Try a station wagon, roof racks or a little inconvenience. So your kids have long legs? Where are these kids with the two-metre legs? The only place I've ever seen them is in the Moomba parade and I thought they were actually normal-sized people on stilts.

So let's get this party started and crack open an icy-cold can of facts, shall we? Let's slip into something a little more uncomfortable with the 4WD safety myth.

Research conducted by the Monash University Accident Research Centre has concluded that 4WDs are almost twice as likely to roll than a car, resulting in their drivers being 3.4 times more likely to be killed due to crushed cabin space.

The centre has pointed out that 4WDs "are not subject to the full range of design rules applicable to passenger cars and their derivatives".

A team from Imperial College London and University of Queensland found, after a study of more than 40,000 vehicles, that "4WD drivers were almost four times more likely than car drivers to be using a mobile phone and 26 per cent more likely not to wear a seatbelt". The researchers concluded that 4WD owners take more risks because they feel safer.

The Australian Transport Safety Bureau found that half the 36 children killed in driveway deaths between 1996 and 1998 were struck by large 4WDs. They have also found: "The proportion of alcohol intoxication amongst 4WD drivers involved in fatal crashes

(29 per cent) was higher than for all other types of vehicle." And: "In 4WD crashes involving multiple vehicles, passenger car occupants accounted for the largest proportion of fatalities (64 per cent). 4WD occupants accounted for 18 per cent."

Children are at risk because they are little and these vehicles are high. As far as proximity sensors are concerned, they do bugger all to protect children. According to NRMA Insurance's Robert McDonald: "They only work about a metre from the car, unless you are travelling extremely slowly. Your reaction time is not going to be quick enough to at least not knock someone over before even realising they are there."

In 2005, NSW's senior deputy state coroner, Jacqueline Milledge, recommended that 4WDs weighing two tonnes or more be banned from school grounds and within 200 metres of schools. She also recommended that the drivers be required to hold special licences after five-year-old Bethany Holder was run over by the driver of a Nissan Patrol with a bullbar.

Due to their weight and the bullbars being positioned at perfect head and chest height, drivers of vehicles hit side-on by 4WDs are 26 times more likely to be killed or suffer serious injury than if they had been hit by a standard-sized passenger vehicle, according to ABC's *Catalyst* program.

But apparently they're fashionable. If pick-up at your school is a procession of kids being collected from school in a car the size of a three-bedroom house, you may want to consider the values of that school.

Will it take a 4WD to back over the child of another 4WD owner for these status-obsessed fashion slaves to realise that these vehicles are potential killers?

Here's a cheaper alternative to buying a 4WD. Just buy a normal-sized car and put a sticker on the back that reads: "I DON'T GIVE A STUFF ABOUT YOU AND I VOTE."

SUZANNE EDGAR

Song of the crestfallen pigeon

The pigeon on my window-sill
adores a bird of wood
that gazes from this other side
as if she understood.

Brought here from America,
she wears a perky crest
feathers brown with a hint of pink
adorn her lovely breast.

The pigeon on the outer ledge
believes he woos a dove
and cannot comprehend the glass
that keeps him from his love.

If only I could speak with him
of love's elusive flame
I'd cure his sad obsession with
the bird he cannot claim.

All day he paces up and down
and pecks upon the pane
his doting morse-code plea for sex
like any featherbrain.

PHILLIP ADAMS

My 2UE producer noticed a tendency for me to nod off during interviews. In my own defence, they lined up some boring farts

The world was agog when Ralph Fiennes was sprung having sex on a Qantas flight with an accommodating member of the cabin crew. Fornicating in the flying loo of a flying roo. My response? Not so much prudish as astonishment. Qantastonishment. For how the hell did they do it? Those jet-propelled toilets can barely accommodate a Mickey Rooney, let alone a full-sized thespian and a hefty, heartily hospitable hostie. The mind biggles.

(Oops! Boggles. For some reason I suddenly thought of the books of Captain W. E. Johns. Biggles and Archie squeezed into their cockpit. Sharing a joystick.) This sort of thing seems an occupational hazard on Qantas. Consider the fact that on another QF flight I slept with Janette Howard. And we don't even like each other. Here's how it happened. When Mrs H flies on official business with Mr H they enjoy the convenience of Australia's version of Air Force One. It's nothing like as comfortable as the Bushes' Boeing, though not too bad. But when the PM's busy schedule means he has to stick around, Mrs H must return with the lower orders on a scheduled flight. And on two occasions, both on the Brisbane/Sydney run, some wag at Qantas has plonked us side by side.

The first time we looked at each other aghast. And, being chivalrous, I suggested that we seek reallocation. Which was, with some difficulty on a full flight, organised. But last time I was too tired for the rigmarole and said, "Don't worry, Mrs H, I'm going to pass out anyway." And putting on my little eyemask, I did.

With a shameful lack of discretion or gallantry, I went on air two hours later and announced that we'd slept together. Yes, I'm a bounder and a cad.

I've also slept with the Greek Minister for Culture. That splendid actor Melina Mercouri (*Never on Sunday, He Who Must Die, Topkapi*) had been given that high office when democracy returned to Athens after the overthrow of the colonels. She was on an official visit to the many Greeks of Melbourne at a time when I had the preposterous title of president of the Victorian Council of the Arts—and I was required to take her to the opening night of a Wagner opera. She was suffering jetlag from another Qantas flight and began lightly snoring as soon as the curtain went up. So I joined her until the interval, when we roused from our slumbers for drinky-poos with the dignitaries.

Despite my training as a theatre and film critic I often sleep through screenings and performances. But it's Qantas's fault. Arriving in London I had to go straight to the West End for *Evita*, and slept through the whole thing. Don't Snore For Me, Argentina.

Ditto through the opening screening of a sequel or prequel of George Lucas's *Star Wars* in New York. Having queued for hours to get in, everyone around me clapped and cheered from the first chord of the familiar theme, but I instantly lapsed into unconsciousness. For which I was extremely grateful, as I needed the sleep and detest Lucas movies. The only reason I went was to write a column on the "*Star Wars* phenomenon". Star Wars, star bores. From Skywalker to sleepwalker. The only phenomenon is how anybody manages to stay awake during these ponderous, soporific epics.

To be fair to Lucas, my own humble presentations also put me to sleep. At 2UE, my producer noticed a tendency for me to nod off during interviews. In my own defence, they lined up some boring farts as interviewees. And at the ABC I sometimes fall asleep during our opening theme. Well, it is a latenight program, so the listeners are asleep, too—and many of my international guests are groggy because it's 5am for them. Or after midnight.

Though a lifelong insomniac who can't get to sleep in beds, I go to sleep in cars, whether driving or being driven. Dr Karl's stern TV admonishments about micro-sleeps while motoring are wasted on me. I have macro-sleeps in taxis and, behind the wheel, like to drift off on long trips. Three cheers for cruise control.

But the worst place for narcoleptic behaviour is, for me, the meeting. Who needs sleeping pills when you've got an agenda? I'm out to it during "the minutes of the last meeting". And, having chaired many a board, it's been a bit of an issue. Meetings go better when the chairman's awake, banging his gavel and shouting "Order!" Or at least asking if someone wants to move a motion. Whereas I've invariably drifted off.

I had various tricks. Like leaning forward and putting my head in my hands so as to look a) heavily burdened by my responsibilities; or b) deep in concentration. But those light snores betrayed me. And the noggin slipping from my hands and hitting the boardroom table was a dead giveaway.

S'cuse me. Need a nap.

SHAUN MICALLEF

My father sat on Winston Churchill

It was 1943. My father had just been voted the prettiest boy in
Gozo.

He was 4 years old and, judging from the crumbling photographs he still insists on showing everyone, looked rather like Shirley
Temple.

His duties were to act as a mascot during the Gamm ta'
L-isfargel Quince Festival. This mainly involved climbing a step-
ladder and pinning St John the Apostle badges onto members of the
Civil Service while dressed as Little Lord Fauntleroy. But on Saturday
he also got to receive any VIP guests arriving at the Port of
Marsaxlokk.

During the previous year Malta had earned the highly dubious
honour of becoming the most heavily bombed place on earth.

So said a plaque fixed to a giant monument of Valettian
limestone which, for at least 12 months, enjoyed the irony of being
the only piece of construction in Malta not reassembled from rubble.
Both Hitler and Mussolini had dive-bombed, torpedoed and strafed
the small clutch of Mediterranean islands with everything they had.
I appreciate they didn't do it personally, but my guess is they were
responsible for it somewhere along the line. For the Axis powers,

the country was a stepping-stone to the oil fields of Persia. For the Allies, Malta was the keystone to victory in North Africa.

By the year's end though there was no food, no fuel, no ammunition, no roads and nowhere to live. My father and his family were actually sleeping in a cave. For their troubles the Maltese were awarded the St George Cross. Just the one though.

Presumably they all got to wear it on some sort of roster basis.

By the next Christmas things would be very different. Italy had surrendered, rebuilding had begun, the quinces were bountiful, rabbits could be heard singing (although only according to Crazy Joe Muscat, the town lunatic) and arriving at the Port of Marsaxlokk on the evening of the 24th were Winston Churchill, Franklin D. Roosevelt and King George VI. They disgorged from their launch armed with gifts for the populace (toys for the children, cigars for the menfolk and lingerie for the ladies), waving and smiling and getting covered in what they took to be confetti but was in fact desiccated coconut stolen from the stores of the USS *Ohio* before it was scuttled. There to greet them was an impressive concord of local dignitaries headed by my 4-year-old father. He got to shake hands with the King of England and was given a pair of silk stockings by President Roosevelt. The stockings later found their way into my great-grandmother's Christmas stocking, which must have been confusing for her.

A lavish civic reception was held at the most magnificent mansion in all of Malta, the Torre Dei Cavalieri. The King was a big fan of bel canto opera and it had been arranged for Maria Callas to sail over from Greece and sing selections from Donizetti, his favourite.

Unfortunately, she couldn't come for some reason and so my father, a precocious child even then, took her place. The fact that he couldn't speak Italian, let alone sing it, did not, on his telling, detract from the fun of the evening.

"I just la-la-la-ed," he says proudly today. Apparently His Majesty very much enjoyed my father's scat version of Lucia di Lammermoor and did not at any stage of the evening ring up Hitler and ask him to resume bombing. I can only assume that the sound of Donizetti spinning in his grave like a turbine carried sufficiently from Lombardy to drown the whole travesty out.

It had been a wonderful night; wine had flowed, legs had danced and the travails of '42 had been, if not forgotten, then politely not mentioned. But the evening was not over yet. Roosevelt stood up and tapped his glass for attention. An aide leaned into him and reminded him he was in a wheelchair. Roosevelt quickly sat down again. He announced:

> My friends, for many months we have wanted to pay some little tribute to you who have contributed so much to democracy, not just here but all over the civilised world. In the name of the people of the United States of America, I salute the Island of Malta, its people and defenders, who, in the cause of freedom and justice and decency throughout the world, have rendered valorous service far above and beyond the call of duty.
>
> Under repeated fire from the skies, Malta stood alone, but unafraid in the centre of the sea, one tiny bright flame in the darkness—a beacon of hope for the clearer days which have come. What was done in this island maintains the highest traditions of gallant men and women who from the beginning of time have lived and died to preserve civilisation for all mankind.

Rapturous applause filled the room and then, just as it started to leave, the President turned to King George VI and nodded that it was his turn. His Majesty removed the blow-tweeter from his mouth.

"Ditto," he exclaimed. The petering applause continued on its way out with barely a look over its shoulder. "But tonight," continued the King in an effort to salvage the moment, "Christmas comes to Malta!" With a majestic sweep of his hand he gestured to the door and who should stagger in but Santa Claus himself.

Churchill, dressed in a long red fireman's coat and straw beard, was distributing candy canes to the clamouring children.

A photographer from *It-Torca*'s social column wanted a picture and Churchill was happy to oblige.

He pulled up a gherkin barrel, plucked my father from the crowd, sat him on his knee and beamed at the camera. The flash bulb burst, startling my father a little and his head shot back into Churchill's chin with a crack. Ash from Churchill's half-smoked Romeo y Julieta brushed against the ostrich feather in my father's Fauntleroy cap, igniting it. The alarm was consistent with that which would greet the sight of a votive candle, but Churchill was nothing if not a man of over-reaction.

Like a rapidly uncoiled jaguar he sprang, seeking to extinguish the flickering plume with the nearest available liquid, which regrettably was in the brandy balloon he was holding.

Fortunately, velveteen is naturally flame retardant and so my father's head was spared any major damage, although he never did manage to regrow his full crop of golden curls and was thus never again to feel within his grasp the prize of being Gozo's prettiest boy.

In fact, 63 years later he's now as bald as a doorknob. Not due to Churchill so much as male pattern baldness. Still, he'll continue entering. Hope springs eternal.

And God bless us one and all.

JULIA ZEMIRO

Idle hands make for short nails

Father's Day, 1982. Year 8. I won't see dad 'til Sunday morning. He's at the restaurant, cooking, sweating, feeding 60 people a night. I will wake him Sunday with my gift, an Ella Fitzgerald cassette tape.

But it will be a little awkward. I have been caught shoplifting during the week and dread having to wish him a happy "father of a juvenile delinquent" day.

Of all the weekends Father's Day—how humiliating. I am not afraid of what my dad will do, but what he will think. And what did I steal? False nails, of all things. This will be excruciating. He has fired waitresses for having false nails. Women who tried to balance three plates of food with long, painted claws.

Idle hands he calls them. Just seeing those talons dipping in the soup or a seafood casserole is enough to make you scream.

Well, your daughter is a criminal with idle hands that got busy nicking stuff. I also stole a packet of chocolate chews. I am tubby enough as it is. No need to gild the lily there.

1982. A time when shop security was, well, non-existent. I am actually a kid who chooses to stay away from trouble. Never expected to get caught but that 65-year-old shop detective nabbed me good. I thought she was an old granny. Talk about your undercover.

Sunday morning comes. Up at dawn, I watch *Thunderbirds* and Gene Autry the singing cowboy, make Milo, put on my roller skates and flail about the back lane 'til it's time to wake dad.

Roller skates still on, I walk up the stairs using the rubber stopper at the front to balance myself. Carrying a breakfast tray with a mug of real coffee, milk and two sugars, two pieces of toast and a beautifully wrapped Ella Fitzgerald cassette, I quietly open the door. I have always loved waking my dad with breakfast. I am a food and drink alarm. As soon as I wake him, and say "Bonjour, papa", I burst into tears. Somehow he knows. My stepmum has worded him up.

He gives me that look you hope a parent will always have for you: "You done wrong but I love you anyway."

I blubber my excuses: I have never shoplifted before, it was my first time, I'm sorry: that kind of thing. And I'm not bunging it on. The shame I feel is real. But of course I have shoplifted before. Mainly nail polish, lipgloss and lollies.

Then dad does that thing you wish parents wouldn't do: he gives me a parallel story of his own stealing escapades.

1946. France. Dad is eight. He steals apples from a next door neighbour's tree and is chased off the property by a farmer, his gun and a dog.

I don't feel better. He and his friends were stealing because they were hungry. I, the tubby teenager, stole so that I may have beautifully long fake nails for a school dance to attract a boy. Highly unlikely, but one lives in hope.

Dad loves his cassette and the coffee's good and strong. I am a chef's daughter, after all. Correct measurements are in my blood.

Dad talks me through the "stealing is bad" speech. And the fake nails? Don't get me started on the idle hands song and dance that followed. But he sees my remorse. Later, he will take photos of me roller-skating in my leg warmers.

The next day, mum has to do the hard yards as we front up to the department store's manager, Mr Pyke. We are there to plead my stupidity. Mum does her best "I'm a teacher, I understand teenagers" speech. She assures him I will be grounded.

But Mr Pyke isn't satisfied. He wants more. Tarring and feathering, maybe? Mum adds more punishments that she can dole out. And he's still not convinced. What's he after?

Then it clicks. My mum the genius gets his drift: "And I can assure you that when her father sees her, she will be severely dealt with." And we are free. She has said the magic word—father. For Mr Pyke, dad means punishment.

Odd. I thought dad meant love. And short, clean nails.

DAME EDNA EVERAGE

My loyal subjects and possums! A seasonal message from President Edna

Like most refined young women of my generation, I was brought up with a beautiful picture of the little princesses on the wall of my Moonee Ponds boudoir. Admittedly, it was just a colour page torn from the *Australian Women's Weekly* and in those days it wasn't as beautifully printed as it is now, so that the colours were a bit smudgy and overlappy. However, it was a gorgeous study of the young soon-to-be-Queen Elizabeth, even though she had about three pretty, smiling mouths running up her cheek like flying ducks on the wall. Whenever the newspapers wrote about Lilibet, they always described her as "radiant", which worried me because I thought it meant radioactive. They also always said she was "smiling happily" too, as though there were any other way of smiling, for heaven's sake!

She was my childhood inspiration and I little dreamt we would become close friends and find ourselves, nearly half a century later, in the kitchen of Buckingham Palace dunking bickies in our tea and sharing intimate secrets like Carrie Bradshaw and Samantha in *Sex and the City*. No prizes for guessing which one of us is Samantha!

The recent Australian elections have got her very excited. "Will little Mr Rudd really turn Australia into a republic?" she asked me this morning with a quiver in her voice. "Pray God, let it be true and I won't have to go on any more of those boring official visits and be groped by your rough-hewn prime ministers or shake hands with those little botoxed Sydney socialites wearing too much gold."

I reassured my friend the Monarch that it was almost certain that the Dentist (as I affectionately call Mr Rudd) would certainly have the republic high on his agenda. "He's not called Kevin for nothing," I added, and we dissolved into peals of laughter, which even woke the corgis under the table and might also have disturbed grumpy old Phil.

When I was last in Australia giving private and confidential elocution, etiquette and deportment lessons to Julia Gillard, she hinted pretty broadly that I was their first choice for president. "Let's face it Edna," she said in her distinctive drawl, "you are impartial, globally respected, beautifully spoken and yet politically to the left of Genghis Khan. Who, apart from me, has better qualifications for the job?"

Julia then went on to quiz me about my royal friends, about Camilla and Fergie and Wills and Princess Michael of Kent and naughty little Harry, with the eagerness of a star-struck schoolgirl. It was a far cry from her public image and I am proud to reveal an unexpected, private side of this formidable little minx.

I'm spending Christmas in Australia this year. First, a visit to the cemetery to buff up my late husband Norm's obelisk. Horrible, dysfunctional vandals from broken homes have scribbled on the Everage mausoleum with their spray-cans in that ghastly chubby writing that seems to be universal. There are uncalled-for words like "expatriate Edna go home" and yuckier epithets, impugning my stance on Iraq, the hostages, discrimination against same-sex marriage in Aboriginal women's prisons and female circumcision in Sydney's southern suburbs.

On Christmas Day, I'll be visiting my daughter Valmai in her correctional facility, which I am dreading. Half an hour staring at the fruit of my womb through a wire-mesh screen, trying not to look at the tattoos on her knuckles. Those little dimpled knuckles that once reached up to me from her bassinette. Christmas dinner will be spent with my son Kenny and his room-mate Clifford Smail, who are both overjoyed by the new government. Cliff is secretary of his local branch of the Window Dressers' Union and he is very grateful to Mr Rudd for giving him back his clout and credibility. He's always wanted the option to pull the plug on Myer's Christmas windows if the in-store Santa continues to be selected according to outmoded gender stereotypes. He wants to nominate his sister, Zena, who is already blessed with ruddy cheeks (no pun intended) and a naturally downy countenance.

To all my subjects, a Merry Christmas and a joyous heart always,

Dame Edna

Politics

KAZ COOKE

Phwoarr, check out the policies on Julia Gillard

Julia Gillard, it's said, has four strikes against her as a possible leader of the ALP. Never mind that only three strikes will see you off the field in baseball, a strategic game made extra fun by sneaking to the next base, secret signals and, in my case, sleeping with the coach. But I digress.

I don't know what the ALP brains trust, which by now must be four blokes and an urn, is thinking. Surely they can't have many members or much more than $2.50 left. And Kim Beazley has about as much chance of being elected prime minister as an iceberg lettuce.

Last time I voted in a federal election, I was so thrilled there was an alternative candidate to the ALP and the Liberals in my electorate I tried to vote for her twice. Anything to avoid going for the mob who took away poor people's right to have decent teeth, or for the ones who let them get away with it.

Telling the Labor Party faction-fanciers that Beazley can't win seems about as effective as a lecture on manners and common decency from Senator Bill Heffernan. Under Beazley, the ALP is like an elderly labrador. While the Government is taking away so many workers' rights it makes you wonder when oxygen will be listed as a perk, the labrador opens one eye and farts like a sigh, its paws twitching in dreamlike reverie.

Sorry, where was I? Four strikes against Julia Gillard. She's a Victorian, she's from the left of the party, she's a woman, and she doesn't have a husband and kids.

Imagine if she did have a husband and kids—they'd be hounded by the media while she was accused of neglecting her family to do her job. Not like all those absent fathers in Parliament who couldn't tell you their kids' favourite colours, the drama teacher's name or what their offspring had for tea last night.

While being a man in Parliament is apparently a get-out-of-town-free card for buggering off and poncing about sounding important while their wives get on with the sticky and exhausting end of bringing up children, apparently it's somehow compulsory for women in Parliament to have kids.

I don't know whether Miss Gillard knows one end of a bub from the other, and I don't care, although I bet she's quite experienced with tantrums. I like her joke that she can't remember what colour her real hair is because she's been dyeing it so long. Lots of women will relate to that.

Brace yourself for the thinly veiled accusations that Gillard is frigid, or slutty, or bats for the other team. It's got to be one of the three, doesn't it? Or, phwoarr, all of 'em!

Kim Beazley won't admit he's a dirigible that's snapped its moorings, full of warm air, pootling across the sky in increasingly elliptical parabolas of pointlessness. And if the ALP seriously can't consider a new leader because he's not from Sydney and he believes in slightly more social justice than Donald Trump and he's a she, then they may as well tie themselves in a hessian sack and throw themselves in the Yarra right now.

I don't know much about Kevin Rudd, but he seems rather across the AWB business, and, frankly, somebody's got to be. He's keeping his head down and travels with his own testicles, so there's much more chance of him suddenly strolling into the lead position, like that gold medal–winning Olympic skater did when everyone else in the race fell over.

Please, Australian Labor Party, the country is begging you. Get a new leader. Choose Rudd or Gillard, or a compromise—Molly Meldrum's a bloke with a girly name. Let the new leader pick their own team regardless of which stupid faction they belong to, then make like a rottweiler and go after that smirkfest they call the Liberal Party.

For God's sake, Tony Abbott's in charge of women's health. Somebody, do something.

GUY RUNDLE

The right wing

Hidden in the NBC archives is a lost episode of the hit series *The West Wing*.

Scene one

Late at night in the Lodge, the Prime Minister's advisers gather.

ADVISER 1: Two weeks after the invasion of the Northern Territory and we're still flatlining. We invaded Afghanistan—score. We invaded Iraq—gold. The Solomons, Timor and in six weeks Iran—all great material. We invade our own country—and nothing. These polls are dead.

ADVISER 2: What does Newspoll say?

ADVISER 1: Don't know. Don't read much fiction.

ADVISER 3: We've got to do something or we're cactus. We need entirely new ideas; an entirely fresh team. We need a bunch of political geniuses the likes of which we've never experienced.

ADVISER 2: Now you're talking fiction.

ADVISER 3: You speak truer than you know.

There is a blinding flash of highly theatrical light and smoke and when it clears some of the advisers from The West Wing—*Sam, Josh, Toby and Leo—are revealed, dazed and confused.*

TOBY: Vertigo. I've got vertigo.

42

JOSH: You're getting vertigo?

TOBY: I said I've got vertigo from the shazam whatchammacallit meshuggenah.

LEO: People ...

JOSH: Sam, Toby's got vertigo.

LEO: People.

SAM: You've got vertigo?

West Wing *adviser CJ enters, dazed, from another room.*

CJ: Hey, has anyone else got vertigo?

TOBY (*shouting*): Yes, I've got vertigo.

CJ: OK, you've got vertigo.

LEO: People, can we forget the vertigo?

JOSH: Easy for you, you don't have vertigo.

LEO: Is everyone all right?

JOSH: Yeah, as far as I can tell our dialogue style remains unaffected.

SAM: Where the hell are we—looks like the early 1950s.

ADVISER 1: Welcome to Canberra. I'm senior political adviser to John Howard and at phenomenal expense to the management we've acquired your services for the duration of the election campaign.

JOSH: Canberra? We're in Canberra?

SAM: Canberra we're in.

LEO: We're in Canberra?

CJ: What's a Canberra?

TOBY: Apparently, what we're in—Canberra.

ADVISER 2: Yes, um, do you always do that—only the election's in three or four months and we'd quite like to crack on.

ADVISER 3: Yes, we all admired the way you turned around Jed Bartlet's re-election campaign through an application of stern principle and an appeal to the best that is in the population and we'd like you to help John Howard win an election exactly in that fashion, except in reverse.

TOBY: Win their election.

SAM: Their election they …

ADVISER 1: Please, really don't start.

LEO: You do understand that we're … fictional? I mean, we're Democrats but we're not real people.

ADVISER 2: Yes, just like our Democrats.

LEO: Gee, I don't know.

SAM: I don't know either.

TOBY: Know? Who knows?

ADVISER 1: Christ, I wonder if this was a good idea.

ADVISER 2: The PM's coming.

John Howard enters. Despite the fact that it is 10.10am, he is wearing a burgundy patterned dressing gown and bearing a cup of Horlicks. He makes his way to an old Genoa armchair in the centre of the room.

PM: Well good morning and how is everybody this morning nice sort of weather we're having isn't it a nice sort of weather I said to Janette that's the wife I said to Janette this morning nice sort of weather we're having this morning and she said yes it would be if it doesn't rain but I said it'd be good for the farmers and the hydrangeas of course and she said John is that a statement of policy and I said what about the hydrangeas and she said no about the farmers and I said yes I suppose it is and she said well if it is going to rain I better get your spencers off the Hills hoist and I said yes you better had because you don't want your spencer re-wetted after it's been dried it'll give it that sort of yellowish tinge which is a shame because a good spencer can last you a lifetime and really there's nothing worse than a damp spencer. Mind you there's nothing better than a dry spencer. Have I mentioned that we're occupying North Queensland next week? Actually who are these people?

ADVISER 1: Um, Prime Minister, these are the new team of advisers we hope will win us the election.

PM: Really? Why are their mouths hanging open?

ADVISER 2: They're just amazed at the opportunity they've been presented with.

PM: New advisers, hey? Do you think they understand Australian culture?

ADVISER 3: Well, they come from American television, so they sort of are Australian culture.

PM: Well, um, wonderful to have you aboard. I've got to go and have a snooze before my nap. Could someone draft up a regulation confining Aborigines to the cattle stations they work on? I'll see you all later. Do help yourself to Horlicks. It feeds night starvation, you know.

And he is gone.

ADVISER 1: Well?

LEO: Gee, I don't know.

TOBY: Know? What's to know.

ADVISER 2: Sorry, what's the problem?

CJ: It's just that we've never met anyone who's more tediously repetitive than we are.

Josh calls from a corner.

JOSH: Hey everyone, it's all right—I was just reading this Fairfax newspaper and in between the sex blog and the guide to the best Tex-Mex cuisine in Phuket there was this actual news story. We can work with this guy.

ALL: Really.

JOSH: Yeah, he's one of us—he's a liberal.

Scene two

The White House. The Oval Office. President Bartlet is writing on a card.

PRESIDENT: Res ipsa loquitor mens rea ars longa vita brevis. Do you think that's enough, Charlie?

CHARLIE: For an eight-year-old girl with leukaemia, more than enough, Mr President.

PRESIDENT: You know what's funny, Charlie?

CHARLIE: That this show is written by Hollywood liberals yet the only regular black character is a 21st-century Step'n' Fetchit?

PRESIDENT: No, it's that, well, let me put it the way I did to the Swedish academy when I won my Nobel.

CHARLIE: Which one, Mr President?

PRESIDENT: Physics—the second one; in Sanskrit it goes … hang on, Leo should hear this. Leo!

MRS LANDINGHAM (*on intercom*): He's not here, Mr President.

PRESIDENT: Mrs Landingham? Aren't you dead?

MRS LANDINGHAM: Still very much here.

PRESIDENT: You were dead last episode.

MRS LANDINGHAM: That's because Channel Nine plays them out of sequence.

PRESIDENT: Where's Leo and Toby and Josh and CJ?

MRS LANDINGHAM: They're on an exchange. We've got their opposite numbers.

Lynton Crosby and Mark Textor enter.

PRESIDENT: Good morning, gentlemen or as Schopenhau …

CROSBY: Cut the shit, you lefty arsewipe.

TEXTOR (*through intercom*): Hey, grandma! Hold the calls! Right—let's kill the rest of the Indians.

Scene three

The Lodge.

TOBY: Meshuggenah this, guys, meshuggenah.

LEO: He did what?

ADVISER 1: He said that he didn't want people who threw their kids overboard in this country.

SAM: But they weren't throwing their kids overboard!

ADVISER 2: Yes, well, I think you'll just have to appreciate the validity of the differences of our political cultures, if you don't mind.

JOSH: You know, President Bartlet had just this problem with a group of Chinese Christian illegal immigrants in series three. He told the National Guard to stand down so they could escape from the detention camp, thus preserving freedom and diplomatic relations.

What does your guy do?

ADVISER 3: Locks 'em up till the kids start cutting themselves.

SAM: Aren't cultural differences wonderful.

TOBY: What kind of shmo is this nebbish? Can we do anything with this shmendrick?

SAM: What's the matter?

TOBY: Yiddish. I'm all out of Yiddish. This guy has de-yiddished me. This guy has de-yiddished me!

LEO: Calm down, Toby.

TOBY: Calm down?! It's easy for you to say, calm down. You're written without mannerisms!

SAM: Could we get back to the matter at hand? This guy we're working for has invaded the Northern Territory.

JOSH: So?

SAM: So, it's the Northern Territory. Of this country.

JOSH: Oh, I thought it was just one of those African countries we invent for shit to happen in from time to time, like the Republic of Mugunga or Equatorial Bong-Bong.

SAM: No, apparently it's a real place—like Montana, only the white people are even crazier.

JOSH: I always wanted to invade Montana, you know. It would solve our problems in the third congressional district.

SAM: Yeah, then we could move Jackson on the armed services committee.

LEO: Which would free up a place on ways and means.

ADVISER 1: Stop, stop!

TOBY: What, what? For chrissake, what?

ADVISER 2: You're being too multi-layered.

ADVISER 1: This is Australian television.

ADVISER 3: You just gave out more backstory in four lines than the entire last series of *Stingers*.

ADVISER 1: Listen, you're not really giving us what we need. What's the problem?

JOSH: Yes, well, usually you see, we're all arguing about some knotty detail of policy and President Bartlet kind of floats in and listens to what everyone has to say and then says something gnomish and lateral, with a few quotes usually starting from Thomas More and going via way of Aeschylus to the Ayurveda *Upanishads* about the great wheel of life in order to lay bare the radically transcendental and redemptionist base to American liberalism.

ADVISER 2: Then what happens?

SAM: Same every episode. We bomb the shit out of somewhere. Usually fictional—somewhere that's been made up as the pretext for something we want to do.

LEO: Like Kosovo.

JOSH: So, can we get that? Huh, what can the PM give us by way of inspiration? Something from *Paradise Lost*, *Urne-Buriall*, maybe? A little burst of the *Lusiads*?

ADVISER 3: Are you familiar with a thing called *Wisden*?

SAM: So, no inspiring quotes then?

ADVISER 2: We do have a bloke a bit like that—name of Bob Carr. Closest thing Australia's had to a philosopher king for a long while.

LEO: Right, so now he's busy helping humanity?

ADVISER 1: No, he got a job with the bank he'd previously hired to build toll roads.

There is silence.

TOBY: Right, so at least give us the minor character dying. At least!

ADVISER 2: Of course. (*Into intercom*) Maria could you get Bill Heffernan over here?

The PM enters in dressing gown carrying steaming coronation mug of tea.

PM: Oh hello everybody sorry I'm late I've just been watching the tea steep and I had an idea—which rather took the fun out of it but I think it's a winner. Let's attack the unions!

LEO: The unions? Why?

PM: Because membership has fallen to 20 per cent of the workforce.

JOSH: So, what you're suggesting is that in an era when no one pretty much joins anything, we allow ourselves to be fooled by their proportional decline and attack the body that has the single largest membership of any social institution whatsoever?

PM: It's getting results.

TOBY: Who for?

PM: OK, how 'bout this? Kevin Rudd when he was a child didn't live in a car or if he did he didn't for nearly as long as he said he did.

JOSH: Didn't ... live ... in ... a ... car.

SAM: For nearly as long as he said he did.

TOBY: Anything else?

PM: Julia Gillard?

LEO: Illegal shares? Sex scandal? She kill someone? What?

PM: She's kind of whiny. (*Silence.*) You know Crosby and Textor would have loved this stuff.

SAM: Crosby Textor, why does that ring a bell?

JOSH: Two guys of those names were executed in Texas this morning.

PM: I think we're home and hosed, don't you?

CJ: Of course.

JOSH/TOBY/CJ/SAM/LEO: President Bartlet!

There is a blinding flash of light and President Bartlet appears, with Charlie.

PRESIDENT: Greetings all or as Nietzsche said "Chock chock tish tash chock", rendered of course in the click language of the Kalahari Bushmen which I presume I have no need to translate. Do I, Charlie?

CHARLIE: Don't ask me, Mr President, I thought your dentures was loose.

PRESIDENT: Charlie, how come you can say anything to me?

CHARLIE: Because I occupy the archetypal role of the Fool in this series—ain't that wonderful? All's I need is a banjo and tap shoes. Mind you, I'd rather be anything but a fool but I wouldn't want to be a Hollywood liberal.

PRESIDENT: I think what we can say is that from the citizens of one new country to another the world will little note nor long remember what we did here, especially if we were up against *Big Brother*. But that these are the times that try men's souls, the summer soldier and the sunshine patriot will in this crisis shrink but that if we are our nations to be the last best hope of man or we are to honour not the old dead tree but the young tree green we must say that independence is our happiness, our country is the world and our religion is to do good, then we shall eventually find out what it was all for and that government of the people, by the people, for the people, shall not perish from the Earth. And if everyone's got a tear in their eye I think it's time for *Lateline*.

Theme music begins.

PM: Times that try men's souls—you know I think you and I might have the same desk calendar.

Cut to living room, viewers watching closing credits in dressing gowns stirring Horlicks.

VIEWER 1: Well, wasn't that a nice night's entertainment?

VIEWER 2: That stuff Bartlet said—it was all bull, wasn't it?

VIEWER 1 (*sighing*): Pretty much—but it sounds a lot better than comfortable and relaxed.

MUNGO MACCALLUM

The pollies went a little crackers

The morning walk is what we'll remember best: that daily ritual which started as a harmless exercise routine, then morphed into a defiant demonstration of the continuing vigour and virility of an ageing, bald, myopic, partially deaf contender.

As intended, it drew the television cameras, with their inevitable following of supporters and opponents. What had been a solo performance turned into a daily spectacular with full-on audience participation.

Naturally the log-rollers and satirists seized their opportunity, and we had a few weeks of theatre of the absurd before the arena was swamped by full-blown loonies and exhibitionists. By the end, the walk had become wholesale theatre of cruelty—a bit like the entire election campaign, really.

John Howard was not the only player strutting and fretting his hour upon the stage: he had an all-singing, all-dancing supporting cast, with a generous sprinkling of stuntmen and clowns. But essentially it was all about him, and his increasingly farcical attempts to elevate what turned out to be a pretty mundane sitcom into something approaching high drama.

In hindsight, the tragicomic denouement was obvious from the time the polls settled in favour of our hero's unlikely antagonist, a fresh-faced man with a plan. It was not so much that Kevin07 became an object of love and affection as that he was just something different. Without noticing, Howard had passed his use-by date, and there was nothing he or anyone else could do about it. But, being Howard, he refused to accept it; he might be mired in the merde, but he remained undeterred.

He had been written off before, but sooner or later the mob had been bribed or frightened back to their senses. Surely the tactics that had worked in the past could be made to work again. So, in the manner of Field Marshal Sir Douglas Haig in World War I, Howard spent the year hurling his (or, rather, the taxpayers') resources into the fray, regardless of cost, in increasingly frantic and always futile efforts to break the enemy line as measured in the opinion polls.

Send forward a revolutionary water plan. Cost: $10bn. Gains: Nil. Enlist a new education foundation. Cost: $5bn. Gains: Nil. Mobilise the troops to take over Aboriginal settlements. Cost: $10bn. Gains: Nil. Hit them with the big one: hitherto irresistible tax cuts. Cost: $34bn. Gains: Nil. Finally, call up the reserves: the great launch offensive. Cost: $10bn. Gains: Nil. And all the while keep up the advertising barrage in an unrelenting assault on the public purse. Cost: $1m per day. Gains: Well, you've got the picture.

The whole campaign cost (or would have, if the bills had ever come in) something more than $65bn. It was not totally wasted: over 12 months, the Liberal vote revived by just over two percentage points. This meant the party managed to avoid annihilation; they saved sufficient territory to regroup for another try in three years. But it need hardly be said they comprehensively lost the war.

The madness of it (in the clinical sense) was that, although from time to time Howard talked about changing his tactics, he never actually did; he and his demoralised army just went on pushing against the door clearly marked pull. The themes were unchanged:

WorkChoices good, unions bad, you can trust me, you can't trust him. Second verse, same as the first, a little bit louder and a little bit worse.

What do you mean the mob's stopped listening? They have to listen. It's their job to listen. They must be joking with us. Or perhaps they've gone off to live in an alternate universe for a while and will come back to Earth on voting day. Be reassured by our friends in the media, who say the polls defy reality, they can't be happening. I mean, Professor Paul Kelly says political reality is inside the beltway and people have moved outside it, whatever a beltway might be. That must mean something. Well, doesn't it?

This chronic refusal to accept the facts led to some wonderful instances of paranoia, one of whose victims was the Channel 9 worm. Howard had always loathed this innocent invertebrate, and its appearance, against his express wishes, sent him into paroxysms of horror. Unfortunately, the feeling appeared mutual: at his every statement, the worm retreated to the depths, while the mere sight of Rudd caused it to leap like a gazelle on steroids.

Rudd was so pleased with the worm's performance that, campaigning at a school the next day, and asked to paint an elephant, he elected to paint a worm instead. The young girl wanted to call it Samara; Rudd christened it Ted.

The ever-alert Tony Abbott deduced that the worm was clearly fixed: it was an anarchist annelid, a new left nematode, a filthy socialist crawler. But of course it wasn't; it was just another opinion poll, albeit a more immediate and graphic one. Once again, the Liberals declined to emerge from their state of denial.

There were flashes of insight: shortly before announcing the election date, Howard blinked his way out of his fantasy world just long enough to ask his colleagues if, just possibly, he might be a teensy-weensy part of the problem and they would prefer him to piss off. Obviously he expected a raucous rejection of such an absurd proposition.

When his loyal envoy Alexander Downer replied timidly that actually, while they all loved and admired him, truly they did, there was just a kind of a sort of a feeling that it might be better if he stood down, he went off to consult his family, or at least the bit of it that talks. Janette apparently advised that she was not going to leave Kirribilli House one second before she was forced to, and that was that.

Howard then embraced the worst of both worlds by saying he would hand the leadership, which he clearly believed was his own private property, to Peter Costello in 18 months or thereabouts. He also said he and Costello would campaign as a double act, but of course they didn't. Howard continued down his own doomed path while Costello did things like attending a children's teddy bears picnic and explaining to a five-year-old that God created cacti.

Eventually, maddened by relevance deprivation, he came out screaming that Australia was faced by an economic tsunami. Howard said it would only be a little tsunami and he could save us. Costello was taken away and sedated and soon afterwards Howard started talking about himself in the third person. Mark Vaile skateboarded down a footpath in Tweed Heads with a baseball cap on backwards and Tony Abbott abused a dying Australian folk hero. Malcolm Turnbull whined to his colleagues in obscene terms about Howard's refusal to sign Kyoto and was accused of leaking the story for personal advancement.

Finally, Howard and Costello did appear together on a commercial television chat show, where they were invited to say nice things about each other. Howard said Costello was clever and funny (implication: Howard wasn't) and Costello said Howard was a hard worker (undoubted fact: Costello wasn't).

Meanwhile, Rudd marched steadily forward from one FM radio station to another, being asked about the colour of his underpants by people with names like Miffy and Daffy and Cobber and Rowf. Having secured the post-adolescent vote when an old home video showing him eating his own earwax was revived and became a bigger hit than *The Lord of the Rings*, he dived into the nearest telephone booth and re-emerged as Super Scrooge, a crusty old skinflint who could be trusted not to spend your savings—on political advertising, anyway.

Julia Gillard, portrayed by the government as Rudd's own Madame Defarge, became—at least for the duration of the campaign—more like Ben Bolt's Alice, the most dutiful and meek of helpmeets. The only break in the calm was when Peter Garrett lurched phallically into the picture and had to be treated with cold showers and bromide.

Rudd still found time to shadow most of Howard's promises and movements: in one memorable hour, both leaders managed to molest the same long-suffering infant in the same shopping centre. Howard accused Rudd of too much Me-Too; Rudd replied that this was just another scare campaign, and proved he was very different by unveiling a visionary policy whereby Western Australians could use their profit from the mining boom to set up as entrepreneurs and sell land in Latin America to wealthy Chinese. When Howard's best reply was a grant of $500,000 to Indonesian orang-utans, his defeat was inevitable.

Rudd won in a landslide—a conservative landslide, as it turned out—but he had always said he was a conservative. Or some of the time, anyway. And Howard went off on his morning-after walk. Even when it was all over for him, he couldn't break the habit of a lifetime.

FRANK DEVINE

All is not lost when you can see success in anything

The British journalist and author William Shawcross once described me in a book as a "cheerful right-winger". Though welcoming the portrayal, it left me with a Zen puzzle: was I cheerful because I was a right-winger or a right-winger because I was cheerful?

The fact that I am cheerful following the election of a Labor government favours the second option, I think.

It goes without saying that we right-wingers require no government support to stay aloft. We are cultural knights rather than political infantry. The lavish skewerings and tramplings of political correctness we enjoyed during the Howard years have left us pretty jaunty.

Our spirits are further elevated by Kevin Rudd moving so close to us culturally, in order to win an election, that there is some talk of clearing a place for him at the Round Table.

In *The Daily Telegraph* in Sydney, our brother Tim Blair caused a small frisson by pointing to the pleasure that awaits us from being able to blame everything on Rudd.

However, there is no prospect of our festering with Rudd-hatred in the way that the sauvignon blanc sippers (chardonnay has become a bit déclassé) of the Left pumped themselves up and made themselves miserable by hating John Howard for a dozen years.

Self-evidently, the less we have to blame Rudd for, the more agreeable our lives will be. However, we'll probably get a kick from watching some natural enemies suffer in the grip of *scheissenbedauern*, a German word that means distress at seeing things turn out well.

Radical Greens have panicked at the prospect of their dreams of post-Howard life going wavery. On the day he was appointed Environment and Arts Minister, they called for the dismissal of the quasi-Quisling Peter Garrett.

Not only had he been ideologically quiescent during the campaign but he had climate change and water supply taken away from him and placed with a new ministry briefed for serious action.

As well, the second arm of Garrett's portfolio might be interpreted as a cruel hint from the Prime Minister that defending frog habitats, overgrown eucalypt forests and weeds from attack by dams, desalination plants, farmers, mines, airports and highways is less a noble cause than a tributary of showbusiness.

While unproductive, Rudd's signing of the Kyoto agreement will cause a severe depletion of the Greens' whingeing resources and devastate their self-righteous posturing.

We haven't heard from the neo-Rousseauians yet but their pain will be a treat to observe when they wake up to the extent of their disarmament by Rudd's apologising to Aborigines for past injustices.

We of the cheerful class are most pleased by the unhurried way the Prime Minister is approaching the withdrawal of combat troops from Iraq, in planned consultation with the US. This is, indeed, a matter calling for prudence. It's one thing to remove fighting men from a losing campaign, another to have them scurry away from an onerously won prospect of success.

Many people may wonder where the war in Iraq has gone, since there has been hardly any media coverage or pundit commentary over the past two or three months. Perhaps coincidentally, this period has seen a significant turnaround of the conflict in favour of our side.

Industrious prowling through cyberspace delivers reliable accounts of the reinforced American military (and their 550 Australian comrades) routing al-Qa'ida in Mesopotamia and damaging and frustrating home-grown militias sufficiently to turn local populations against them. Violence has been notably reduced in Baghdad. Iraqis who fled their country are starting to return, a reported 46,000 in October alone.

The New York Times, the most ferocious of anti-Bush, anti-war campaigners, has largely let the war slide from its front page, after it dominated for five years. In compensation, *Times* commentary has dwelt, until a month or so ago, on political progress not following military success.

However, Shia and Sunni appear to be seeking accommodation. The Iraqi government is rehiring relatively large numbers of Sunnis who were ejected from public service jobs after the fall of Saddam Hussein. Though parliament has not yet passed a law specifying a system for distributing oil revenues among the provinces, the government is fairly equitably handing over the money.

Of profound strategic significance is the government's reportedly favourable attitude to permanent US bases in Iraq.

With a dainty turn of phrase, *The New York Times* notes that US presidential candidates are seeking "tonal adjustments" of their Iraq positions. After wavering for a long time, Hillary Clinton declared herself anti-war when the Democrats won a congressional majority a year ago. The latest Rasmussen poll shows her trailing leading Republican candidate and war supporter Rudy Giuliani.

With the schadenfreude prospect of watching some awkward clearing of the throat by our own proclaimers of American humiliation in the morass of Iraq, it's no wonder I'm cheerful.

MARIEKE HARDY

Er, thanks for your support. No, don't call us, we'll call you

"I would like to keep our place like it is and I guess (joining the) Liberals would be natural." This was the important announcement this week from a colourful and in no way unhinged Sydney resident, Kate McCulloch of Camden, after she had successfully prodded at her local council to reject a proposed building site for an Islamic school.

This, of course, was after she'd appeared on television wearing an oversized Akubra hat that had Australian flag postcards stapled to it like a misguidedly patriotic entrant in a primary school parade, blithely referred to our general Muslim population as "the ones that come here", and then rounded off by declaring that famous colonials John and Elizabeth Macarthur would no doubt be on Team McCulloch were they a) alive and b) remotely concerned with local education-based planning issues. She certainly couldn't be accused of being dull.

What the Liberal Party made of her coy public flirtations can only be a matter of speculation. Presumably they spent the ensuing hours changing their locks and answering the phone using a comedy accent and repeating the words "Brendan Nelson? Nobody here by that name, sorry", though this is, of course, guesswork.

Who knows, perhaps a wild-eyed maverick with a fondness for controversially divisive politics and potentially slanderous quips may be just the thing they're looking for. Wilson Tuckey won't live forever, you know.

With folk like Tuckey and McCulloch in mind, I'll proffer this alarming truth: you can never hand pick those who appoint themselves as mouthpieces for your particular cause. And more's the pity, too. No doubt there were a small number of Camden residents who may well have opposed the Islamic school solely on planning grounds and would have quietly preferred rabid "get orf my land" types like McCulloch to shut the hell up and let them handle things, but those few, it's sad to note, never made it to the papers. What was that Groucho said about not wanting to belong to any club that would have you as a member?

As a young lady with left-leaning tendencies, I'm far happier when the acerbic wit of comedian Jon Stewart steps up to bat for my side, rather than the interminable musical stylings of John Butler. It could be an entirely personal thing, but a well-timed satirical knock-knock joke seems able to prick a few more consciences than an eight-minute marimba solo.

Bill Hicks is infinitely preferable to the caterwauling of the Dixie Chicks, Stephen Colbert is hands-down more punk rock than Rage Against the Machine will ever be, and Chris Martin from Coldplay seems a nice enough chap but should almost certainly stop writing about coffee beans all over his hands and just play the piano.

Michael Franti's another sanctimonious prig the left may be relatively pleased to get rid of. If I see one more interview where he pads around barefoot proclaiming to be a "citizen of the Earth" I'm going to stab someone. Why can't he be a spokesman for baby-kicking and identity theft? At the very least I'd feel less guilty about throwing things at him every time he busts out that tepid bumper sticker rhyme, "We can bomb the world to pieces, but we can't bomb it to peace." Right-wing redneck homophobic logging whale-killer extremists: take our Franti. Please.

In terms of conservative comedians you've got the inherently amusing Ann Coulter, creator of such outstanding zingers as "My only regret with (Oklahoma bomber) Timothy McVeigh is he did not go to *The New York Times* building" and, "It would be a much better country if women did not vote." Last I heard she had a sold-out run at the Hammersmith Apollo with her one-woman stand-up show *AmeriKKKa's Most Wanted*. Or wait, maybe that was Ice Cube. Anyway, she's no doubt doing wonders for the cause.

The same can't be said of the vast majority of Stormfront members who appear to have trouble with spelling, no doubt sadly setting the cause of white supremacists back a couple of decades or so, and I don't know whose side serial pest Peter Hore is on, but if he ever professes a love for literature and the Tote Hotel in Collingwood, I'm switching teams.

Musician Alice Cooper's a rabid conservative, a fact that no doubt thrills Mr and Mrs Middle America, particularly when the one-time Vincent Furnier wraps himself festively in long-suffering boa constrictors or pretends to hang himself on stage while wearing make-up.

Who in their right mind would want their personal politics represented by a man who once sang the words, "Thrill my gorilla/ Where were you when the monkey hit the fan?"

At least Johnny Ramone made decent music and had a nice haircut. And in the end, isn't that all you want from the spokesperson of your cause? Someone offer Mrs McCulloch a cup of tea and a sit-down—she's inflicting some major damage.

GUY RUNDLE

Don't worry, just testing

1. Ban Ki-Moon is:
   a) New secretary-general of the United Nations.
   b) A character in the *My Little Pony* series.
   c) Both of the above, following a widening of the search for candidates.

2. Australian of the Year was:
   a) Tim Flannery, for tireless campaigning on global warming.
   b) Ben Cousins, for going for rehab to LA.
   c) Lisa Robertson, who did Ralph Fiennes for nothing on a Qantas flight, the only time a passenger gave complimentary nuts to a hostie.

3. Princess Mary of Denmark gave birth to a daughter whose half-Australian ancestry was recorded in her name:
   a) Christiana Frederika Beatrix.
   b) Astrid Katarina Gertrud Ophelia Elke Katarina Hentzau von Schlewsig-Holsteinette.
   c) Jaidyn.
   d) Astrid Katarina Jaidyn Katarina.

4. Widespread drug use in the Tour de France was established among:
   a) The Kazakh team, after they failed random testing.
   b) French competitors, after confessions.
   c) The audience, who couldn't possibly be watching a month of cycling at 3am, straight.

5. The Federal Government sent the army into the Northern Territory because:
   a) It wanted to address social dysfunction in Aboriginal communities.
   b) It wanted to experiment with retaking state governments by armed force.
   c) It had run out of foreign desert nations to screw up.

6. Tony Blair resigned as British Prime Minister in order to maximise the chances of his preferred successor:
   a) Gordon Brown.
   b) David Cameron.
   c) St Paul.

7. Kevin Rudd published an essay on the German theologian and martyr Dietrich Bonhoeffer written in difficult and uncompromising English because:
   a) Confusion about ALP position on Protestant conception of Trinity really hurt them in 2004.
   b) Still some doubt whether glasses, diplomatic career and smug grin might have absolutely and totally alienated him from voters.
   c) Magazine wouldn't accept the Mandarin version.

8. Britney Spears' skimpily clad comeback appearance on the MTV awards reminded people:

a) That she could still rock out when she wanted.

b) That stardom will often take a terrible toll.

c) To clean out the oven grease-trap.

9. President-elect Nicolas Sarkozy was unusual for French politicians in:

a) His commitment to free-market policies.

b) His pro-Americanism.

c) Waiting till his wife left him before shagging everything in sight.

10. Glenn Wheatley was sentenced to a jail term for:

a) Tax evasion.

b) That John Farnham farewell tour.

c) The slack bass line on "Turn Up Your Radio".

d) Perception by some that he's a bit of a dick, though it sounds better in legalese.

11. Paris Hilton announced she was going to Rwanda for:

a) A fresh start after her prison sentence.

b) To draw attention to global suffering.

c) Diet tips.

12. The sentencing of Carl Williams to 35 years' prison assured people that the only gangsters left in Melbourne were:

a) Safely on the screen, in *The Sopranos*.

b) Too busy running the ALP right to disturb anybody.

c) Out of a job now the drug squad's been abolished.

13. President Pervez Musharraf declared a "state of emergency" in Pakistan to perpetuate his power by any means, provoking in the US and Australian governments:

a) Strong condemnation.

b) Mild condemnation.

c) Great interest in the process of implementation.

14. Russian journalist Alexander Litvinenko was served food glowing bright green in a British restaurant, leading to suspicions:
a) That he was being poisoned by the Russian Government.
b) That he was being poisoned by the Russian mafia.
c) That he was the only person in the country whose lunch had any flavour.

15. Australian footballer Ben Cousins announced that to undertake rehab for cocaine and other drugs he was going to:
a) Los Angeles.
b) Bolivia.
c) Angelo's House de Crack, Mogadishu.

16. The fake news team who managed to get into an APEC meeting were:
a) *The Chaser* team.
b) The Fox News network crew.
c) Jackie Kelly's husband, in a dry run.

17. The outbreak of equine flu resulted in:
a) Cancellation of several race meetings.
b) Concern about Australian veterinary procedures.
c) A public clamour to ban all immigration from Equinia; exposé of their queue-jumping, disease ridden ...

18. John Howard's loss in the 2007 election was due to the fact that he lacked:
a) The public affection enjoyed by Peter Costello.
b) Alexander Downer's common touch.

c) Brendan Nelson's reputation for depth.

d) The cojones of Vladimir Putin.

19. Following the election, Peter Garrett was relieved:
    a) Of responsibility for climate change.
    b) Of the role of answering environmental questions in Parliament.
    c) That he didn't have to dance like a freak on another Midnight Oil tour at the age of 55.

20. Prime Minister Kevin Rudd announced to the world that the nation would offer an apology for:
    a) The stolen generations policy against the Aborigines.
    b) Supporting the 2008 nuclear attack on Iran.
    c) The achingly obvious symbolism in *Jindabyne*.
    d) Joe Dolce's unaccountable failure to deliver a follow-up to "Shaddup You Face".
    e) Three sodding more years of the same.

Big shout out to my man Sean Dooley for the disgustingly sexist Ralph Fiennes joke.
ANSWERS: Oh, come on.

Society

MARK DAPIN

Adventures in LA-Land

Britney Spears tried to force her way into my hotel late last night. This is not the sort of problem I normally face, but this week I am staying at the five-star Raffles L'Ermitage Beverly Hills. Apparently, Britney (she's always Britney, never Spears) first attempted to check into the nearby Four Seasons, but was turned away because she was being chased by an incandescence of paparazzi. She ditched her car in the hope of sneaking into L'Ermitage, but the hotel was full. Had she succeeded in getting a room, it would have been the worst attempt to escape the press in the history of Los Angeles, since staying at L'Ermitage for an E! channel, pre–Golden Globes international press week are almost two dozen celebrity-watching journalists from around the world. And me.

Before I was invited to LA, I did not know what E! was (I thought it was a show; it is a channel); I did not know what the Golden Globes were (I thought they were TV awards; they are movie and TV prizes granted by the Hollywood Foreign Press Association); and I did not know what the Hollywood Foreign Press Association was (but that is okay, because nobody else does, either).

I quickly learn that E! specialises in celebrity gossip and reality TV. Its best-known show in Australia is *Girls of the Playboy Mansion*, which purports to chronicle the supposedly polygamous life of Hugh Hefner and his three blonde consorts. During the week to come, we will interview Hef and many other stars of E!'s highest-rating reality shows and ask them what can be done about Britney.

I have a luxurious "smart room" at L'Ermitage and, predictably, it is much smarter than I am. When the room turns on background music, I cannot turn it off.

Once I have persuaded my room to let me out, I join journalists from Italy, France, Spain, Brazil, Germany, *OK* magazine and Adelaide in L'Ermitage's breakfast room annexe to await the arrival of the Kardashians. I do not know who they are, either.

It turns out they star in the E! show *Keeping Up with the Kardashians*, and they are LA fashion-industry identities of indeterminate ethnicity and perplexing celebrity. The three daughters—Kim, Kourtney and Khloe—are the children of the late Robert Kardashian, one of O. J. Simpson's trial lawyers, and their mother, Kris, who performs in infomercials. Kris is now married to former Olympic decathlete Bruce Jenner, who also makes infomercials.

Mother and daughters are dark and sultry and dressed entirely in black and white. Before they file into the interview room, E! PR consultant Paul Gendreau asks how many of us have had a chance to catch their show. Nobody raises a hand.

Consequently, the first question the Kardashians face is about Britney.

Britney, apparently, has said Kim has an "amazing figure". What is her secret?

"I work out a lot," reveals Kim, "but my New Year's resolution is to eat a little better, because I eat way too much sugar."

"Kim actually just finished shooting her new work-out video," says mom Kris, infomercially. "And it'll be up on officialkimkardashian.com."

The key word here is "official". There are many Kim Kardashian sites on the internet, but most of them point to a 30-minute hard-core sex tape made by Kim and her then boyfriend

Ray J, a rapper and actor who is known for neither his rapping nor his acting.

The tape, *Kim Kardashian Superstar*, is notable for its unusually high production values, and looks more like a pilot for a series than Kim's friend Paris Hilton's single-camera tragedy. Episode one of the first season of *Keeping Up with the Kardashians* deals with Kim's mortification about the sex tape, and her appearance on *The Tyra Banks Show* to talk about it. In a later episode, she attempts to put the notoriety even further behind her by posing nude for *Playboy* magazine.

E! has barred questions about the sex tape, so there is not much to ask the Kardashians.

What kind of a man does Kim like?

"I think that now I definitely want someone who has a really good body," she says, "who's really fit. I've dated people who haven't, and now I'm like, 'What was I thinking?' I'll never, you know … look back."

Like *Kim Kardashian Superstar* and Kim's support bra, *Keeping Up with the Kardashians* is essentially a vehicle for Kim's breasts. It is only a reality TV show in the sense that it is more real than, say, *Shaun the Sheep* or *Teletubbies*. It feels rehearsed, staged and very badly acted, particularly by Kris, who seems unable to play herself with any emotional authenticity. Similarly, Kim is not a very good Kim Kardashian, which augurs badly for her stated ambitions to star in other, more challenging roles.

~

There are two kinds of people: those who watch pay TV and those who have no idea what the other kind are talking about. Those who watch pay TV tend to watch everything on pay TV, and are the only people in Australia who might have heard of Kimora Lee Simmons, star of *Kimora: Life in the Fab Lane*.

Simmons, a former model, owns the clothing brand Baby Phat, and is the ex-wife of Russell Simmons, co-founder of the Def-Jam record label. Part Japanese and part African-American, she calls herself "a pop culture phenomenon". Much of her appeal seems to rest on the regularity with which she uses the word "fabulous", from which she has derived a new noun, "fabulosity".

Simmons has skin the colour of pawpaw, and licorice hair like a Gauguin muse. She talks about Carla Bruni ("always very fabulous"), Victoria Beckham ("fabulous") and Amy Winehouse. ("I'm not saying she's not fabulous. She's quite fabulous in her own lane. Which is not my lane.")

Simmons does not stop talking, even when her sentence is finished and her idea is clearly exhausted. It is as if she cannot stop, does not know when to stop, has no idea of structure or punctuation or logic. She consistently contradicts whatever she said last, and appears to be speaking not so much to communicate as to drown out the competing voices in her head. When she says "negative" she adds "connotation", even when nothing is connoted. When she says "talented" she appends "bunch", even when she means only one person.

Was she worried about putting her two children on the show? "I don't think my kids know that they're different because they're on TV," says Simmons, "because that's their world. Their nieces and nephews [she means their cousins] have a reality TV show, too."

~

Simmons's niece and nephew star in MTV's *Run's House*, about the family life of Russell Simmons's brother, Rev Run, once a rapper with Run-DMC. Kim Kardashian, before *Keeping Up with the Kardashians*, guested in reality shows *Sunset Tan* (about a tanning salon) and *The Simple Life*. Even her sister Kourtney has appeared in *Rich Kids: Cattle Drive*. When Kim posed for a *Playboy* centrefold, she cemented a link between two competing LA unrealities, the Kardashians and the Playboy Mansion.

The *Girls of the Playboy Mansion* press conference is the only one held off site, at Hef's place itself. The mansion is the expected mix of culture and kitsch, with a Picasso on one wall and a portrait of Hef with three lions on another. There are peacocks in the grounds, and cabin rooms with beds, magazines and tissues, for party guests (but not journalists) to "get to know each other".

Hef appears first. At 82, and dressed, as usual, in his pyjamas and dressing-gown, he somehow manages not to look as if he has just torn out his drip and escaped from the hospice.

He may have had a bit of surgery on his face, and a lot of creative work done with the remains of his hair. It is impossible to say where his part is, and a dark streak that perhaps once grew down from the side of his head now turns upwards and shelters his crown. But he still looks good. He has bedroom eyes, lizard eyes, laughing eyes, and the lines on his face flex then fade when he smiles.

In the savagely compelling show, the jewel in E!'s navel, Hef sleeps with the oldest "girl", Holly Madison, but the two others, Bridget Marquardt and Kendra Wilkinson, live in as his "girlfriends".

"My relationship with Holly is a real one," says Hef. "What you get on this reality show is reality, unlike most reality shows, which have been scripted. The reason we are able to go on despite the writers' strike is we have no writers."

The Writers Guild of America's strike against the Alliance of Motion Picture and Television Producers has caused problems for everyone in the room except Hef. The writers have asked the actors to boycott the Golden Globes awards night. The journalists are supposed to be here to attend the Golden Globes after-party. All over the world, newspaper and magazine editors are wondering why they have dispatched their top writers—and me—to cover an event that looks increasingly unlikely to happen.

The dispute has also had the awkward side effect of focusing attention on the essential nature of the Golden Globes. On movie posters, DVD sleeves and actors' CVs, a Golden Globe seems to have the cachet of an Oscar, but the Oscars are awarded by the Academy of Motion Picture Arts and Sciences, which has more than 6000 members, all of whom are in the movie industry. The Hollywood Foreign Press Association, meanwhile, has 82 members, many of them only part-time journalists. They are not a representative section of the foreign press corps, most are not film reviewers, and, in any normal situation, their collective opinion would be only marginally more important than a consensus among LA burger flippers, or car valets.

Hef says he supports the right to strike but would like to see the dispute settled, and talk soon moves on to the real issue facing Hollywood—Britney.

There were rumours, says a journalist, that *Playboy* asked Britney to be in the magazine and she said no, or that Britney asked *Playboy* if she could be in the magazine, and the magazine said no.

"I think," says Hef, "that there was a period of time—and it is still going on—in which the need to invent stories relating to Britney Spears was everywhere, and all the tabloids and other publications made up stories as they went along."

A journalist asks if there is anywhere in the house the cameras are not allowed to go.

"Well, you won't see me in the toilet very often," says Hef. "We leave the best part to the imagination," he adds, referring to the bedroom rather than the toilet.

Hef wanders back to bed, or wherever it is he spends all day in his pyjamas—and the girls take his place. They are all blondes (of a shade not often found in nature) and big-breasted (of a shape not often found in nature).

Kendra Wilkinson introduces herself.

"I just got my boobs done," she says. "Redone," she amends. "They're bigger, too. Bigger and better. I was going to go smaller but I decided not to."

The journalists are keen to know what the girls' parents think of them being on the show.

"My family loves coming here," says Wilkinson. "My mum just got a plastic surgery makeover," she adds, pointing to her own breasts.

Everybody else in LA seems to see themselves as role models. Do the "girls"?

"We encourage people to work out, get an education, follow their dreams," says Bridget Marquardt.

"Be themselves," says Wilkinson.

"We're not encouraging them all to date the same guy," says Marquardt.

Wilkinson, 22, describes her career to date thus: "I graduated when I was 18. I was a general assistant. I got my boobs done, then—bim!—I'm here."

A reporter wants to know if all the girls' periods are in sync. Wilkinson pulls on the belt of her pants, looks down into her underwear, and says, "I think I've just started mine, actually."

It is Wilkinson who makes *Girls of the Playboy Mansion* so ferally watchable. Like everybody else in LA, she talks all the time but, unlike everyone else, she says exactly what she means. This, oddly, has given her the reputation of being a bit thick.

~

Nowhere is the disconnection between actions and words more apparent than in the press conference given by Dr Robert Rey, one of several cosmetic surgeons who feature in the E! reality show *Dr 90210*. Oleaginous, predatory, handsome, slim and egomaniacal, Rey laughs confidently, nervously and hysterically, talks patronisingly, excitedly and apparently disinterestedly, flirts, flatters, takes us into his confidence ("I'll be very honest with you"), calls us baby, calls himself baby, and at one point appears to refer to a penile implant as "baby".

Rey, the story goes, was born to a poor family in Brazil, and brought to the US by Mormon missionaries.

"Let's start with a question from Brazil," says PR Gendreau. So a Brazilian journalist asks a question in Portuguese.

There are no lines on Rey's face, and there is no fat on his casually displayed midriff. Somebody asks the secret of his youthful good looks. "It's diet!" he says. "Diet and exercise! And happiness! You can decide to be happy and, when you're happy, you don't age!"

This is the first of several bizarre replies that avoid entirely the question of cosmetic surgery and are punctuated with audible exclamation marks.

"Coffee's no good for you!" he declares. "Eat like Palaeolithic people!" he advises. "Spirituality!" he spruiks.

Then he gives a spontaneous presentation about fashions in contemporary cosmetic surgery.

"[Implanted] chins are very popular," he says. "We are androgynising women. The little nose that went like this [he presses his nose upwards], like Barbie, that's long gone. Today, a natural nose is in. I had my nose done so it's a natural look," he says, and I think it is the strangest thing I have ever heard.

There has also been "a shocking increase in butt augmentations", he says. "We do lots and lots of butts: either the Brazilian butt lift [whatever happened to impenetrable Latin names for operations?], which is the transfer of fat from one area to the behind or, for girls too skinny, we put an implant in.

"We're doing a lot of vaaaginoplaasty," he says. He relishes the word, drags it out. "Laaaaabioplasty." He almost flicks it with his tongue. "Women have these beautiful lips down below," he says. "When they give birth, those lips may get dragged down.

"And sadly, sadly—remember, I was brought to America by Christian missionaries—sadly, fashion in sex is unfortunately driven by the porn industry and unfortunately today everyone shaves their genitals. Hair, you don't see any more," he announces. "I've undressed about 11,000 women—about 50 girls per day—and, I tell you today, *no one* is hairy. So what you could hide before, today you cannot hide. So that little extra lip down below now starts to erode the girl's self-confidence."

"It" can be inherited—"from your mom", he adds, help-fully—or it can be a result of pregnancy. Luckily, however, "It can be fixed by a half-hour operation.

"I'm glad plastic surgeons have took over this area," he says. "I've got nothing against gynaecologists, but they're not delicate. They don't care so much about the *looks*. They're just worried about function."

Rey later explains that somehow, bafflingly, a situation has emerged where there are people who want cosmetic surgery but *don't really need it*. Objectively speaking, their butt might already be Brazilian enough, or the nose they were born with sufficiently natural. The reason they might want to change it is as puzzling to Rey as it is to you or me. It is a medical condition with a Greek name: dysmorphia. Rey says this is "a huge problem".

So, what makes somebody beautiful? "Beauty starts from the inside," he says, and advises us to help mothers struggling with prams, after which we will find we "seem to radiate light".

"If you want to erode the inner core, if you want to hate yourself, if you want to have a very bad self-opinion: live one thing, and preach something different," he says.

"I'm going to ask this question for everybody," says Gendreau, helpfully. "Do you feel like putting yourself on TV, and doing what you do, in front of the world, has held you up to a higher standard of ethics? Has it made you a better doctor?"

"I always get the best questions with the foreign press," says Dr Rey, apparently unaware that Gendreau is his PR.

The answer is yes, he does, and yes, it has.

~

There are two kinds of stars, real stars and reality stars. The difference between them is the difference between rapper Snoop Dogg and everyone else we meet over the week. When Snoop enters the lobby of L'Ermitage—fabulously late—he glides across the floor on a sheen of impossibly relaxed charisma, fuelled by joints as strong as his two colossal bodyguards. He must have helped a lot of mothers with their prams, because Snoop glows like an amber light at an intersection.

An interview with Snoop is worth serious money to any jobbing journalist, so we're divided into four groups of six, to make sure nobody in the same market gets the same quotes. Snoop disappears into a room, the smell of burning dope fills the corridor, and an announcement comes through the haze that Snoop will only do two sessions, which means nationalities represented by more than one correspondent will have to double up.

It is fine by me, and almost everybody else, but there are two kinds of journalists: the visiting foreign press and members of the Hollywood Foreign Press Association (whose Golden Globes ceremony has just been officially cancelled). Today we are joined by one of the latter, and she is furious that she might lose her exclusive. The rosters are revised over and again, but it is impossible to cosset her in a room with only Spanish and Hebrew speakers. Eventually, as the appointed hour for the two sessions passes without Snoop emerging from his cloud, she storms out without meeting him, while the rest of us sit or stand or pace, waiting for our 45 minutes with the most honey-voiced, treacle-tongued rapper in the world.

When Snoop finally floats in, his eyes are half closed. He folds himself onto a throne (a throne!) at the front of the room. He is wearing glass beads in his hair braids, and what looks like the gusset of a stocking on his head.

He says he made the show *Snoop Dogg's Father Hood* to present himself to the public in a positive light, not as a playa and a gangsta, but as a loving husband and devoted father.

"I'm a French journalist," announces a woman from the floor. (This is always a sign of a perplexing question to come.) "You're addicted to chicken," she says.

Snoop smiles, as if this were a compliment.

"Aren't you scared to eat all the chicken of the world?" she asks.

This thought is alarming enough for a man who is so stoned that his hair beads are weighing down his head, but there is more to come: it is a probing, two-part question. "What would you eat if there is no more chicken?" the French journalist continues.

"Erm ... if there's no chicken ... " says Snoop, stroking his chin. "I don't know about it. Hopefully, that'll never happen."

It is left to the Brits to give voice to the question on nobody's lips.

"You've had loads and loads of fame," says a man from the tabloids, reasonably, "and, obviously, Britney Spears has gone through nightmares. You've probably met her in the past." He corrects himself. "Of course you have. How do you think she could get herself out of these problems? Is there any advice you could give her, coming from where you've been?"

Snoop looks at his crotch for inspiration.

"Association by affiliation," he says. "You've got to associate with people who are doing the right things in life, and that rubs off on you, you know. If you hang with nine killers, you're gonna become the 10th. You hang with nine doctors, you're gonna become the 10th."

~

On the other side of the world, there is a nation dying in Iraq, another being born in Kosovo, and a premature Kurdistan struggling to breathe in an incubator built by Americans that Americans may yet take away. But none of this seems important—or even real—in Beverly Hills, where only the star-struck, car-crash cacophony of E! channel makes sense, and where everyone—except perhaps Kendra Wilkinson—is acting.

Here in Los Angeles, the big question is not what can be accomplished in Baghdad, Pristina or Mosul, but what should be done about Britney. Should she adopt Kim Kardashian's gruelling dietary regimen? Should she pose for *Playboy*? Should she, as Snoop Dogg seems to suggest, seek the company of nine doctors, in order to obtain medical qualifications by osmosis?

Patently unscripted, barely believable, packed with celebrity guest stars and impossible plot twists, and broadcast on E! all day, every day, Britney Spears is, without a doubt, the best reality TV show in town.

LES MURRAY

Fame

We were at dinner in Soho
and the couple at the next table
rose to go. The woman paused to say
to me: *I just wanted you to know*
I have got all your cook books
and I swear by them!

I managed
to answer her: *Ma'am,*
they've done you nothing but good!
which was perhaps immodest
of whoever I am.

ROY SLAVEN

Seven modern wonders indeed?
I think not

I have just become aware of a list of the new Seven Wonders of the World.

The process of determining the list has totally escaped me, but apparently it was arrived at by democratic means through the World Wide Web.

I've subsequently grilled many friends, colleagues and associates about the new list and, to a person, they, like me, knew nothing about it.

So the democratic process that has delivered us the What's Paris Up To Now phenomenon has determined the new Wonders.

It's no wonder at all, then, that they are just a little bit ordinary.

The Great Wall of China comes in first. Rather than being a wonder it was a massive waste of time, achieving nothing and costing as many lives per metre as a normal month in downtown Fallujah.

While the idea was to keep the marauding hordes from the north out, it never achieved this noble ambition; bribing the gatekeepers put paid to this notion.

And having strolled a goodly section of the wall north-east of Beijing, I can report that much of it looks like it was built yesterday—because it was.

The original wall is all but disappearing out of sight of tourists. Should a failed effort of human folly be considered a wonder? I doubt it.

The ancient city of Petra at number two, however, is quite a nice spot, especially when floodlit at night. But again, I have to compare it with other surviving ancient cities and, if given the choice between Petra and, say, Pompeii or Herculaneum, Petra doesn't quite measure up.

If anyone was serious about getting a feel for what life in an ancient city was really like, they wouldn't go to Petra—even in the old days.

Paul, Peter and John the Evangelist headed off to Ephesus and Corinth because they considered Petra a bit on the dull side.

When you wander down the main street of Ephesus and pause outside the great library, you feel much more in a space of wonder than you do when appreciating the bronze chisel work of Petra.

Machu Picchu is good. If you were going to design a place where you could cut the hearts out of the hapless poor to appease the gods, this is it.

To sit in silence when there aren't too many tourists about and imagine the rivers of blood flowing down the steps, while not all that uplifting, is tremendously sobering, and that in itself is not a bad thing.

Ditto the Mayan ruins of Chichen Itza. Full marks. A top spot for a bloodfest ... a message not completely lost on the Spaniards.

And the same applies to the Colosseum in Rome, which was little more than an edifice to bread and circuses.

Though I think the Pantheon, tucked away as it is behind a shopping strip, is a much more wondrous building.

The Romans were not noted for their subtlety when it came to public architecture, but with the Pantheon they almost accidentally struck a particularly aesthetic note—and a note that still rings wondrously clear today.

Making up the Seven are the Taj Mahal and the big Christ in Rio. In Sydney, the St George Leagues Club is known locally as the Taj Mahal, and given the choice of Tajs to while away a few hours in, I think I'd go with the leagues club. I know Melburnians feel exactly the same way about Windy Hill. There's just a lot more to do at these places.

I'm not suggesting the Agra Taj could be improved with poker machines and carpet on the walls, but the white structure in Agra, while Christmas-cake pretty, I found just a little bit cold.

As for the statue of Christ the Redeemer, it's rubbish—the sort of work that gives kitsch a bad name.

The Greeks probably didn't have a bad idea when they thought up the wheeze of the Seven Wonders all those years ago, but to me the wonder of the ancient world is to where the enlightened sensibilities of the ancients disappeared.

To wander through the archaeological museums of Athens, London or Istanbul is to witness the very highest points of human aesthetics up until 1CE, yet 1000 years later artists were baffled by the simple notion of perspective—a problem not solved again until the Renaissance.

A truly modern set of wonders would have to echo our times and sensibilities—and that necessitates them being pop. For what it's worth, witnessing a Collingwood–Carlton grand final at the MCG is very hard to go past as a modern wonder.

But, then again, finding out that P. Hilton's performance on Larry King was the most watched show since the moon landing causes a very serious pause for thought.

MALCOLM KNOX

Corporatising culture: Who holds the past in common trust?

I am sitting in a car. A taut-voiced woman is leaning into the window, telling me what not to touch.

She points to a battery of buttons flashing across the dashboard.

"Don't touch."

She points to the handbrake, gearstick and pedals.

"Don't touch."

She points to the passenger seat.

"Don't touch."

It is as I set off at 15 kilometres an hour, climb a narrow ramp and approach a sharp left-hand turn that I cannot remember whether she told me not to touch the steering wheel. Will the woman run up to me in my crashed vehicle and say, *I never told you not to touch the steering wheel! What kind of idiot are you?*

I close my eyes, fold my hands on my lap and place my faith in technology. The steering wheel turns itself. I'm away, up hill and down dale, on a lengthy circuit past a ferris wheel, a test-driving track, an educational display, a photography exhibition, a modelled Formula-1 pit stop, an Imax theatre and a rank of race-car simulators. I am tickled pink every time the ghost in the machine turns my steering wheel. Soothing elevator music fills the cabin.

Where exactly am I? It's not easy to answer. This is a place called Toyota Megaweb, situated on Odaiba, an island reclaimed from Tokyo Bay in the heady bubble days of 1988. Odaiba means "cannon emplacements", as this was the fort from which Japan intended to defend itself against Admiral Perry 150 years ago. But the past has closed around us from behind. Odaiba is a futuristic mini-city, and it has the white elephant's obligatory assemblage of monorail, artificial beach and ambitious, forward-looking architecture. Unlike anywhere else in Tokyo, Odaiba has an abundance of empty lots.

The Toyota Megaweb, which I circle in my radio-sensor-controlled "E-com ride car", is a place of paralysing ambiguity. It is certainly a tourist sight: the place is as shutterbug-packed as the temples of Kyoto. As well as the E-com ride, it has the Imax, with seats that convulse in violent Parkinsonian shudders, the simulators, the F1 display and, outside, the ferris wheel. Is it a theme park? There are giant video screens, cafés and a racetrack for children to pedal electric vehicles, but it might also be a science-and-technology museum: the Megaweb contains an interactive educational display on hybrid vehicles and a "Universal Design Showcase" of household items (slogan: "Universal Design: made to make you happy!"). A wall is implanted with every Toyota gearstick and dashboard ever made, each with an explanation of why its design seemed a good idea at the time. And, lest we think this is just about cars, the Universal Design Showcase has furniture, pens, crockery and a model city. Perhaps the Megaweb is a museum after all. It does have a "History Garage" of vintage cars. Incongruously—though I'm not sure if there is any congruity left to mess with—there is also an exhibition of photographs and drawings about John Lennon.

But let's cut to the chase. The hybrid vehicles are for sale. The test-driving track is for prospective Toyota buyers. The Imax and simulators feature great moments in Toyota-racing history. The History Garage is filled only with Toyotas. I can't quite work out the

John Lennon connection, as I thought he was a Rolls fan. But at the centre of the Megaweb beats a very familiar and functional heart: this is a car showroom. Many of the Japanese tourists are ordinary people buying cars. All the free entertainment—everything that has brought me here—is garnish. I am sightseeing in a car yard.

Across town, in the established shopping precinct of Ginza, is the Sony Building. Like the Megaweb, the Sony Building is featured in all of my tourist guidebooks, and it is also filled with tourists who are consumers and consumers who are tourists. The space-age interior is modelled conceptually on the New York Guggenheim, a single path spiralling through the exhibits. As at the Toyota Megaweb, there are interactive displays: you can make a film of a toy town; you can play games on next year's computers. The information desk is unmanned, instead advertising Sony technology by asking you to manipulate a touch-sensitive electronic card and view your hand on a TV monitor.

It strikes me that all high-tech consumer shops could be interactive science museums or computer-game arcades if they wanted to, but Sony has brought this ambiguity front-and-centre. When I sit down before the latest Bravia flat-screen television, which transforms the water of Japanese TV into the wine of compelling viewing, what have I become? Am I a tourist checking out the newest Japanese miracle, or am I a convert to a brand? No salesperson approaches to gauge my interest. They are happy for me to remain uncertain as to what, precisely, I am.

Things get weird when I climb to the twenty-fifth floor of the Shinjuku L Building, across the road from the Park Hyatt, where Bill Murray and Scarlett Johansson loved each other unrequitedly in Sofia Coppola's 2003 film *Lost in Translation*. Here at the Toto Super Space, I am taking a tour of a toilet showroom. Again, "Universal Design" is the proud boast, "applied to all plumbing environments". Toilet-roll holders enable "one-hand, one-touch" usage. Toilets have backrests and remote-control adjustable seat heights. Taps are automatic (in Japan, I don't think I ever turn a tap handle). And, of course, there is the famous Washlet, a Toto trademark that caused a "WC revolution" in 1980 (advertising jingle: "Our bottoms want washing as well"). The Washlet is the toilet that makes a watery sound when you sit on the seat, for ladies' modesty, and doubles as a bidet. There is not much to buy here, apart from toilets, taps and bathtubs, but I can get a souvenir ashtray shaped as a toilet bowl, complete with cistern. I take a very informative free booklet about the historical evolution of Toto's ecological virtues, customer-friendliness and usefulness to society at large, and enjoy the view from 25 storeys.

In Japan, there is every blend and recombination of what is cultural and what is corporate. The Tokyo beer museum is owned by the beer company. The tobacco museum is owned by the tobacco company. There is the corporate showroom as curio (Toto Super Space), and the corporate showroom as funhouse (Toyota Megaweb, Sony Building). There is the company headquarters self-advertising as a theme park (the NHK television and Ghibli animation studios). There are shops which blur their identity with historical exhibits (the Pentax shop has old cameras in glass cases, and the Leica shop has a photo gallery, old cameras and even, in its repairs section, a case of cameras destroyed in disaster or war—irreparable!). The Pen Pilot showroom, Pen Station, displays the evolution of fountain pens through the years. Art galleries are either name-branded (the Bridgestone Gallery is one of Japan's foremost) or they form a floor of existing shops (the cosmetics house Shiseido has one floor dedicated to art exhibitions). The media conglomerate Axis has set up a corporate/cultural centre in which it is impossible to distinguish the exhibit from the retail. In Shibuya, an Audi building is being fitted out, promising customers a place "to come in and experience our brand". Not buy a car, but experience the brand.

Sometimes it is the building itself that makes it into the Lonely Planet or the Frommer's. Prada, Comme des Garçons and Louis

Vuitton, among many others, have commissioned structures which attract architecture students; tourists flock to the bubbled, diamond-panelled Prada building in Aoyama. As advertising, it is cost-free.

But what does it all mean, and why is this intermarriage of the corporate and the cultural so arresting? I find myself pressed by the same question that has been pressing for the half-century of the Japanese economic miracle. Am I seeing a harbinger of the next century or a new permutation of the past one? Which of this will travel: which is just weird Japanese stuff, and which of it is our future? And why does it all make me so uneasy?

~

When I was young, no school trip or holiday with friends through the Hunter region, north of Sydney, was complete without a visit to the Oak Factory. Oak milk was then a regional phenomenon: you didn't get it a hundred miles south. Being regional, it was exotic. At the factory, we took the tour. Not quite Willie Wonka, but pretty good: a factory that turned the disgusting stuff that squirted out of cows into cold chocolate milk. After the tour, when we were taken into the Oak shop, we discovered that Oak milk tasted fresher, better, sweeter than ordinary milk. No milkshake could ever match (nor has it ever matched) those bought at the Oak Factory milk bar. Now that the Oak Factory is a wing of Dairy Farmers and Hungry Jack's, Oak milk is everywhere and it doesn't taste like anything.

All this is to say that the commingling of factory, shopfront and advertising is neither new nor oddly Japanese. What are our beautiful wineries but Oak Factories for grown-ups? The invasions and deceptions of advertising were much more blatant in the industry's early years—the medicinal qualities of Coca-Cola, or the way Don Bradman turned himself into a human billboard for his endorsements—than they are now. Like fast-adapting bacteria, corporations are sneakier and more potent. The sandwich-board guy has turned himself into the guy paid to drive a Nando's Chicken car around town. Advertising has colonised names—remember Garry Hocking, the Geelong footballer rechristened, for a handsome commission, Whiskas?—and the 3 corporation can patent a number. Even time itself can be sold off to an advertiser. In an eerie life-imitating-art moment, an American football team started its first match this season at 7.11 pm, the publicity an ample payoff for the cheque written by its sponsor, 7-Eleven. It made me think of David Foster Wallace's 1996 novel *Infinite Jest*, set in, respectively, The Year of Glad, The Year of the Depend Adult Undergarment, The Year of the Tucks Medicated Pad and The Year of the Trial-Sized Dove Bar. A decade ago, Wallace thought he was joking.

Australian corporations have for years been colonising tourism and leisure spaces, from AMP's purchase of naming rights over the highest observation tower in Sydney to Telstra's brand-takeover of the Olympic Stadium, nee Stadium Australia. Art galleries, opera companies and museums are used to singing for their supper. The money for blockbuster exhibitions has to come from somewhere, and for every quid there is the pro quo of naming-rights sponsorship. Culture morphs into retail: the museum shop is now a necessary little earner, and it's not simply for museum and gallery visitors but for locals wanting to drop in for a funky or arty gift.

So much for the shop attached to the museum. What of the museum attached to the shop?

Our companies have tended to be more modest than Japan's. They keep their art collections securely in the boardroom, for the edification of staff and important clients. No Australian corporation worth its salt *doesn't* produce a handsome coffee-table book on the company's history, but these are produced to enhance the company's prestige among insiders and clients. Seldom are these vanity items projected to the public, and seldom does the public show any interest. If Channel Nine turned its studio into an interactive theme park, like Tokyo's NHK network, would anyone come?

Although Australian companies will try to get their names on sporting gear, zoos and theatres, the sponsor is still understood as parasitical on the cultural exhibit. It's not like Japan, where a Toshiba rugby team, playing in the top division, was traditionally made up of Toshiba employees. (Or it hasn't been like that, in Australia, since our cricketers earned enough not to have to work as salesmen for Benson & Hedges when they weren't on the field.) If we were like Japan, all those Friday-lunchtime office soccer teams would be the A-League.

The seamless knit of corporation and culture plays up to our preconceived ideas of the Japanese as a nation of salarymen, company drones. *Lost in Translation* could scarcely squeeze in character and story amid the product placement. I don't know if Suntory paid the real Bill Murray to go to Tokyo and advertise its whiskey, but the fictional beverage company which paid Murray's fictional character is actually a real company that sells real whiskey. Coppola has said that this is just the point: it's impossible to depict Japan realistically without stuffing it with product names.

Let's follow our intuition, then, that in Japan, culture and corporation, leisure time and sponsored time, privacy and advertising, have undergone a complete merger. Let's also assume that this is not a Japanese invention but rather a typical example of the Japanese way of sampling, absorbing and naturalising what it has learnt from the West. (This explanation, by the way, carries a particular conviction for me: I am in Japan for a symposium on jury systems; Japan is adopting a jury system for its criminal courts in 2009; my attendance stems from the thorough-going Japanese effort to study and cherry-pick the best features from every other jury system around the globe.)

Let's also say, out of an instinct for the way our society is headed, that the merger of corporate and cultural is so profitable and productive that it cannot help but spread around the world. And let's ask, is there anything wrong with that? Are our feelings of unease going to be outmoded, slipping into Australia's memory like communism and religious sectarianism?

My reflex is to say, with the automatism of anyone born before 1970, that of course it matters. The Not-For-Sale sign on our culture, our families, our personalities, our time, must stay up. But the argument needs constant restatement and rethinking. Does it *really* matter if the National Gallery becomes the Telstra Gallery or if BHP's collection becomes Melbourne's most-visited Australian-art gallery? Does it *really* matter if my infant children can't say "3" on its own, but instead say "3 mobile"?

I feel vigorously that it does matter, yet I also feel myself resembling Chip in Jonathan Franzen's *The Corrections*, who teaches college students how to critique their popular culture but is floored by the student who retorts, "Nobody can ever quite say what's wrong exactly. But they all know it's evil. They all know 'corporate' is a dirty word. And if somebody's having fun or getting rich—disgusting!" This precipitates a crisis in the liberal-arts teacher:

> Criticising a sick culture, even if the criticism accomplished nothing, had always felt like useful work. But if the supposed sickness wasn't a sickness at all—if the great Materialist Order of technology and consumer appetite and medical science really was improving the lives of the formerly oppressed ... then there was no longer even the most abstract utility to his criticism. It was all, in Melissa's word, bullshit.

The "evil" in corporate mergers with cultural spaces, therefore, has to be re-argued continually to an audience who suspects, like the gen-Y Melissa, that "what's so radically wrong with society that we need a radical critique, nobody can say".

~

After I return from Japan, the air is thick with talk about "Australian values". Everybody wants to talk about what they are, but nobody argues that values, whether national or familial or personal, are less nouns than verbs. Values aren't what we know, but how we do things. And our values are expressed in how we process what comes to us from the outside. It shows up in the discussion about how we treat asylum seekers and other immigrants, but it's also part of how we process those imports that don't need to apply for a visa.

To generalise, there are two ways an object can migrate across borders, and it's much the same whether we're talking about an idea, an art movement or a widget. One is because it's needed. The small, cheap, fuel-economic car was needed; the Pachinko machine was not. The microchip was needed; the Washlet was not.

The other way is when nobody sees any reason to resist the import. The question moves from "Why?" to "Why not?" This accounts for the bulk of our cultural imports. Nobody needed the Walkman or sushi, but once they were on offer, there seemed no good reason not to adopt them. This is how the meshing of corporate and cultural will happen, is happening. Some bright spark will visit the Toyota Megaweb, a light bulb will flash, and next year we will have dodgem-car rides, Daytona simulators and an electric-car exhibit at the most profitable car showroom in Perth. We will ask "Why not?" and come up with no answer that doesn't make us sound like a stick-in-the-mud. It's an Australian value to welcome ideas when they pay their way, when they sound like fun, when they do no harm. We've never closed our borders to the economically productive person, product or idea. We've never stood on our dignity, culturally, which is why we have been such a fertile market for consumables.

Just how ripe we are strikes me a week after I come back to Australia. I go away for the quintessential summer holiday: two weeks in a sleepy, one-shop coastal village. The shopkeeper is building a new tiled patio in front of the fish-and-chips counter. One day, I walk past and he's standing there, admiring the tiles. I say, "You can't let anyone walk on that. Just admire it." He says, "That's right—just like the ad!" Then I remember that his stance did indeed remind me of a TV ad. I thought I was being witty, but instead I was parroting an advertiser's witticism. The shopkeeper mentions another, similar, ad. We have a whole conversation about ads.

Many of us are always having conversations about advertisements, whether we know it or not. Ads link us by way of shared jokes, lessons, myths, ways of seeing, much as our ancestors were linked by their holy books or folklore. Advertising has taken over from religion in providing that invisible web inside ordinary conversations. So does it matter if our culture—an outcrop of our conversations and our thoughts—sells itself to the advertiser?

The other thing happening in this seaside village is that everyone is up in arms against a new development. The council has agreed to sell off public land to a real-estate developer, and the locals' reaction is to put up posters accusing councillors of taking bribes and "destroying the way we live". Not just a few hectares, but an entire way of life is deemed to be at stake. Everywhere on our coast, from Sydney Harbour to Broome, we have huge tracts of land that belong to and are used by the public. It seems particularly Australian to hang onto so much prime land for the public good. Although we're a soft touch when it comes to the privatisation of our minds, we are deeply hostile to the privatisation of what we can see and touch: our land. We are a materialistic people. We worship the material world. You can buy up our art, but you leave our beaches alone. So where does our history fit, on this spectrum between the two-dollar shop of ideas and the Fort Knox of bushland and beach? How tightly held is our history? Do we care enough about it not to sell it to the highest bidder?

It's here—in the ownership of history—that I find why I'm so uneasy about the corporate showroom as cultural exhibit.

In Ginza, Shiseido has two buildings. The Shiseido Gallery is housed in the flagship store, glossily red in the colour of the brand.

Among the perfumes is one floor devoted to rotating exhibitions of the visual arts. The exhibitions have nothing to do with Shiseido, but provide a pleasant accompaniment to shopping. The other building, a few blocks away, is the House of Shiseido corporate headquarters, built in 2004. Inside the headquarters is a museum dedicated to Shiseido history. It's open to the public and is well patronised—as are the Shiseido Corporate Museum and Shiseido Art House, entirely separate edifices situated outside Tokyo. This is one proud company. Its "Corporate Culture Department" was set up in 1990 with this charter: "valuable managerial resources that reflect the intellectual and spiritual outcomes of our corporate activities".

The corporate headquarters' museum, foremost among these intellectual and spiritual outcomes, is both beautiful and informative, with interactive displays and a temporary exhibition, "Women in the Ginza", about professional women working in the area in the past century and a half. I learn that Shiseido was founded in 1872 as a pharmaceutical retailer, turning to cosmetics in 1897. The historical display includes other scenes from Japanese history, such as the country's first beauty contest, held in 1892. So comprehensive is the museum's embrace of Japanese history—Shiseido, it implies, *is* Japan—that I'm curious as to what it says about World War II. I can find three references:

> 1942: The enforcement of container standards makes production of cosmetics difficult.

> 1943: Beauty department closed.

> 1943: Tokyo factory bombed. Young women wear more subdued hairdo.

That is the sum total of the war, through Shiseido's eyes. No Pearl Harbor, no Nanking, no Coral Sea, no Hiroshima. And in recalling this, later, when I'm back in Australia tossed between the sell-off of our minds and the territoriality over our beachside bushland, the penny drops for me.

Of course it's not a company's responsibility to tell the full story. The company only owes responsibilities to itself, its shareholders and its customers. It owes nothing to the national past; if you want to find out about Japan's history, you will have to go elsewhere. But when the private corporations own not only the means of production but also the cultural spaces themselves, where will there be to go? If culture is privatised, aren't we only going to hear the private owners' version? After all, they'll have paid for it. Who will hold the past in common trust? Who will protect our stories as jealously, and guard them as protectively for the common good, as our voters and ratepayers protect our public land? From Tokyo, I can't help but think that the greatest threat to our understanding of the past won't come from leftist teachers in black armbands or Windschuttles in rose-coloured glasses, but from a corporation who will remember the violence of early settlement as a time when land-clearing became more difficult, sales of firearms rose and young women wore more subdued hairdos.

CLIVE JAMES

The perfectly bad sentence

In writing, to reach the depths of badness, it isn't enough to be banal. One must strive for lower things. Almost five years have gone by since I cut out from a British newspaper the article containing the following passage, and I think I am finally ready to examine the subtleties of its perfection. But first, let the reader judge its initial impact: "Now, the onus is on Henman to come out firing at Ivanisevic, the wild card who has torn through this event on a wave of emotion ..." (Neil Harman, *Sunday Telegraph* sports section, front page, 8 July 2001).

Time has elapsed, Tim Henman has dropped out of the top 50 after never sticking long in the top five, the original clipping has gone a mellow colour at the edges, and the featured sentence is at last ready to be analysed, as a fine wine slowly makes itself ready to be tasted. Ivanisevic aside, there are two men involved here: Henman and Harman. One is a tennis player, and one writes about tennis. It is Mr Harman, I think, who is better equipped for his career. Tim Henman was always a bit too lightly built in the chest and shoulders. Mr Harman has what it takes to go on serving his clichés and solecisms with undiminished strength forever. But let's take a look at how he does it—or how he did it, on the day that no spectator of bad writing will ever forget. At this point the reader should scan the sentence once again, slowly, as with an action replay.

An "onus" is a weight, but the word has been so long in the language that its derivation can safely be left for dead: Shakespeare himself would have no quarrel there. For Henman "to come out firing", however, is borderline at best. We can leave it neutral, but would prefer to know why the metaphor is military. Baudelaire, in *Mon coeur mis à nu*, warned us that journalists with a fondness for military metaphors were proving their unwarlike nature. For all we know, Baudelaire's stricture fails to fit Mr Harman, who might have been in the SAS before he turned journalist. We can't help suspecting, though, that Mr Harman has no accurate picture in his mind of what sort of weapons Tim Henman might be firing at Ivanisevic. The writer simply means that the British tennis player is behaving aggressively. But then we find that the British tennis player is behaving aggressively towards a wild card. The wild card, again, is a metaphor that can be left for dead: it was brought in from gambling, but we court pedantry if we ask for it to be brought alive. All we can ask for is that it be not too grotesquely transfigured in its death: the corpse should not be mutilated. If a wild card tears through something, it should not be on a wave of emotion. Suddenly the British tennis player, weighed down with his unnamed weapons, is attacking a wild card that has become a surfer. And the sentence isn't even over.

But neither is its impact, which has only just begun. Speaking as one whose flabber is hard to gast, I'm bound to say I was floored. Not bound in the sense of being tied up with ropes by a burglar, or floored in the sense of having tipped my chair over while trying to reach the telephone with my teeth: I mean floored in the sense of having my wings clipped. One of my convictions about the art of composing a prose sentence in English is that for some of its potential metaphorical content to be realised, the rest must be left dormant. You can't cash in on the possibilities of every word. In poetry you do more of that than in prose, but even in poetry, *pace* Baudelaire, you must concentrate your forces to fight your battles, and there is no concentrating your forces in one place without weakening them in another—a fact that Field Marshal von Manstein vainly tried to point out to Hitler.

To achieve conscious strength in one area, we must will a degree of inattention in other areas: such has been my conclusion from long experience. But here, from out of the blue, is a sentence that demonstrates how the whole construction can be inattentive, and achieve an explosive integrity through its having not been pondered at all. Imagine the power of being that free! Imagine being able to use a well-worn epithet like "out of the blue" without checking up on whether its implied clear sky comes into conflict with a storm later in the sentence, or whether it chimes too well, but in the wrong way, with a revelation in the previous sentence that the person being talked about once rowed for Oxford or Cambridge! Imagine not having to worry about "explosive integrity"! Imagine, just imagine, what it would be like to get on with the writing and leave all the reading to the reader!

Too late. I missed the wave, perhaps because I was carrying too many weapons. A kind of wild card myself, I might have ridden my potato-chip surfboard more easily if I had not been burdened with all my onerous ordnance. The mine detector, especially, was the straw that broke the camel's back—or, as Mr Harman (and Australia's prime minister) might have put it, was the bridge too far. At high school in Sydney I was taught not just to parse a sentence but to make sure that any pictures it evoked matched up. Our teacher, Mr Aked, was not a professional philologist, but like all people with an ear for language he was a philologist at heart. He taught us enough Latin roots to make us realise that etymology was a force in the language, and the more likely to be a confusing force the less it was recognised. He didn't make it all fun. Some of it was hard work. But he made the hard work satisfactory, which is the beginning of good teaching, and I suppose that period was my one and only beginning of good learning: I began to become the student I would be in later years, long after I had proved that formal study was not my gift.

It was also, alas, the beginning of my suffering. My antennae for linguistic anomaly were extended and I could never afterwards draw them in. Even today, half a century later, I can't use a word like "antennae" without first picturing in my mind what kind of antennae I mean. Are they metal antennae, like the basket-work arrays of a radar station, or are they fleshly antennae, as on a bug? Having decided, I try to make something else in the sentence match up, so as not to leave the word lying inert, because it is too fancy a word to be left alone, while not fancy enough to claim its own space. Having finished the piece, I comb through it (what kind of comb?) to look for what I overlooked: almost always it will be a stretch of too-particular writing, where the urge to make everything vivid gets out of hand. But I will still question what kind of urge gets out of hand, and I might even have to look up the origin of "out of hand", to make sure it has nothing to do with wild cards.

Purple patches call attention to themselves and are easily dealt with by the knife. The freckle-sized blotches of lifeless epithet, unintended repetition and clueless tautology are what do the damage. In the first rough draft of this piece, in the first paragraph after the quotation from Mr Harman, I had a clause, which I later struck out, that ran thus: "with the bonus of its proud owner's barely suppressed grief". But "barely suppressed" is the kind of grief that any journalist thinks a subtle stroke; and, even less defensibly, "bonus" echoes "onus", one of the key words of the fragment under discussion. All that could be said for my use of "bonus" was that I used it without tautology. In journalism, the expression "added bonus" is by now almost as common as it is in common speech. (My repetition of "common" is intentional, and the reason you know is that you know I must know, because the repeated word comes so soon.)

Too many times, on the way to Australia by air, the helpless passenger will be informed over the public-address system that his Qantas flight is "co-shared" with British Airways. The tautology is a mere hint of how the Australian version of English is rapidly accumulating new tautologies as if they were coinages: as an Australian police officer might say, it is a prior warning. Already the spoken term "co-shared" is appearing as "code-shared" when written down: I saw it this year at a Qantas desk in Terminal 4 at Heathrow, and Terminal 5 isn't even built yet. If the language goes on decaying at this rate, an essay consisting entirely of errors is on the cards. In the television studio it is already on autocue. (In America I could have said "cue-cards" for "autocue" and got a nice intentional echo to make "on the cards" sound less uninspired, but it would have been unfair: American English is the version of the language least prone to error at present—or, as the Americans would say, at this time.) But when all the nits are picked, and the piece is in shape and ready to be printed, one can't help feeling that to be virtuous is a hard fate. Most of the new errors I couldn't make if I tried. In the Melbourne *Age* of 27 August 2001, an article that it took two women to write included the sentence "The size of the financial discrepancies were eventually discovered." I couldn't match the joyous freedom of that just by relaxing.

What I would like to do, however, is relax my habitual attention to the sub-current of metaphorical content. Most of the really hard work is done down there, deep under the surface, where the river runs in secret. (Watch out for the sub-current and the river! Do they match?) No doubt it would be a sin just to let things go, but what a sweet sin it would be. It is sometimes true of poetry, and often true of prose, that there are intensities of effect which can be produced only by bad writing. Good writing has to lay out an argument for the collapse of a culture. Bad writing can demonstrate it: the scintillating clangour of confusion, the iridescent splendour of decay. A box of hoarded fireworks set off at random will sacrifice its planned sequential order, but gain through its fizzing, snaking, interweaving unpredictability.

The handcart of culture has to go a long way downhill before the hubs wobbling on its worn axles can produce a shriek like Mr Harman's prose. You will have noticed how, in my previous paragraph, I have switched my area of metaphor from chaos to decay, and then from pyrotechnics back to chaos. I would like to think that this process was deliberate, although there is always a chance that I undertook it in response to a reflex: the irrepressible urge to turn an elementary point into a play of fancy. If it is a reflex, however, I hope it lurks in a deeper chamber than my compositional centre, and so leaves room for conscious reflection—a word from the same root, by suggesting a very different tempo.

Mr Harman's reflex occupies his whole mind. But he should worry: look at what he can do without pausing for thought. In his classic sentence, Mr Harman does not commit a single technical error. It is on a sound grammatical structure that he builds his writhing, Art Nouveau edifice of tangled imagery, as if Gaudi, in Barcelona, had coated his magic church of the Sagrada Familia with scrambled eggs, and made them stick. Mr Harman has made a masterpiece in miniature. There is an exuberant magnificence to it. As Luciano Pavarotti once said, I salute him from the heart of my bottom.

SHANE MALONEY

In from a busy day at Barwon jail, Carl asks for a fair go

Come yesterday, I'm whiling away a stray hour in the County Court, watching the fine grindings of the wheels of justice, when into the courtroom comes a certain inmate of the Barwon prison: to wit, Mr Carl Williams, also known as "Babyface" and "Big Fella".

Now, Mr Williams is not a party with whom I care to share a vicinity, on account of what I have read about him in the newspapers, even if it is not all true. Such is his history of discreditable activities, indeed, that he has been enjoying an enforced sequestration from the wider community for the past two years, hence his address.

Bearing in mind the potentially fatal consequences of proximity to Mr Williams, I am immediately tempted to evacuate myself. My nerves are soothed, however, by the presence in court of a quartet of stony-faced jacks from the Purana taskforce, a body of coppers whose dedication to the eradication of criminal violence is legendary. The merest glance from these gentlemen could peel the rust off an iron bar and their leader, Inspector Ryan, is so tough he makes that Mullett chap from the police union look like a member of the Pussycat Dolls.

Positioned safely behind the wallopers, I study Mr Williams as he is led to the dock, a sort of glass-walled corporate box at the back of the room. As his nickname suggests, Babyface is not a man of egregiously frightening mien. With his moo-cow eyes, his bland dial and gormless expression, he could easily be taken for a slightly bewildered first offender on a drink-drive charge. But Mr Williams is not here to face charges of blowing above the limit on Pascoe Vale Road. He has taken time off from his busy schedule to explain to judge Betty King why he deserves the court's mercy as concerns sentencing for the near-total eradication of the Moran family of drug dealers, a crime to which he pleaded guilty at his last appearance before her. These slayings come on top of the bumping-off of a notorious hot-dog vendor and narcotics peddler, a transgression for which he is serving 26 years in the Acacia maximum security unit.

To lend moral support, various members of Mr Williams' family begin to arrive, positioning themselves on the seats immediately below him. For the occasion, his former wife, Roberta, has chosen a fetching yellow beanie which she has teamed with a hoodie and yellow-top trainers. She immediately takes the opportunity to address some disparaging remarks to Mr Williams' current inamorata, Renata, who is seated a short distance away. Renata, who is younger and more blonde, responds with frosty silence.

The proceedings, what with legal argument about what can and cannot be published, take the best part of the day. To begin, Mr Williams' silk, Mr David Ross, QC, reprised the circumstances of the murders perpetrated at Mr Williams' behest. These involved guns of various shapes and varieties, a wheelie bin, large amounts of cash and drugs and statements by the prisoner to the effect that he did not entirely trust the police, that he was taking a lot of self-prescribed medicine at the time and that he was once shot in the tum-tum by Jason Moran.

Judge King, resplendent in red robe and funky specs, reminded him that she had heard most of it before, but she would be giving his plea all due consideration. With that, Mr Williams was escorted back to Barwon, where every day is, in Mr Williams' words, "like Groundhog Day".

Environment, Science and Technology

CLIVE JAMES

On climate change

In my household, I'm the last man standing against the belief that global warming is caused by human beings.

Three women with about a dozen university degrees between them have been treating me for years now as if I were personally responsible for the forthcoming death of the planet. They're probably right. They were right about the cod.

After it was impressed upon me by my daughters that the number of cod in the sea had declined to the point that there were 20 miles between any two cod, I stopped eating cod, and immediately the cod-stocks began to recover.

I couldn't help noticing, however, that there were no complaints about the declining number of haddock.

Since it was crumbed haddock fillets that I took to eating instead of crumbed cod, by rights there should have been a noticeable and worrying decline in the number of crumbed haddock being caught in the North Sea. There wasn't, but if there had been I would have listened to the evidence.

Hard, observable evidence should convince anybody sane. I know the sea is polluted because I can see plastic bottles on the beach. Whether the sea is indeed rising might be a matter for computer modelling, which is evidence only if it suits your prejudice, but you know what a couple of hundred plastic bottles are when they come in riding on a wave like a flock of dead seagulls.

Where I used to go on holiday in the Bay of Biscay in the days when I could still swim over-arm, the empty plastic bottles on the beach were only a few centimetres apart all the way from France into Spain.

I marvelled at the perversity of people on board ships who, after drinking the contents of the bottle, would carefully screw the cap back on so that the bottle would float forever, unbiodegradably carrying its unwritten message of human imbecility until the ending of the world.

Some countries litter more than others. Sometimes the same country litters less than it used to. Australia was a litterbug's paradise when I first left it in 1961. Fifteen years later, when I first went back, the littering had largely vanished, because a government campaign had actually worked.

At present, the same global coffee bar chain has cleaner forecourts in the US than it does in the UK because, in the UK, dropping trash is a yob's right. But wherever you are, in Birmingham or in Birmingham, Alabama, biodegradable packaging in general is clearly a necessary and welcome step, well worth paying for if you've got the money.

The fact that only a very small proportion of the total human race has got the money we can leave aside for now, because this is really about us, the people who can afford to do the right thing after we've either agreed what it is or been prevailed upon to do it by a government which has proved its competence in other areas, such as finding a use for the Millennium Dome.

This week, for a packet of organic tomatoes still gamely clinging to their own little vine, I gladly paid extra because the packaging was almost as enticing as the contents. By means of a printed sticker, the packaging promised to disintegrate at some time in the future.

It would have been a help if the exact time in the future had been specified—perhaps about the time when the last remnants of the human race left for the planet Tofu in the constellation of Organica—but at least the green promise had been made, and I would be able to put the empty tomato packet into our wheelie bin devoted to compostable matter.

In Cambridge we divide our garbage into two wheelie bins, marked compostable and non-compostable.

The two classifications don't apply to the wheelie bins, both of which are made of heavy-duty, non-compostable plastic, but do apply to their contents.

As the dolt of the household, a mere male and therefore little more than a brain-stem with a bank account, I myself am correctly regarded as too stupid to decide what goes into each bin. My job is to substitute one bin for another in the garden shed according to which week which bin is collected.

Only women are clever enough to plan this schedule but only men can do the heavy labour involved, employing the brute force for which they have been famous since the cave, when everything was biodegradable.

A world nearer to a bone-strewn cave is one to which some in the green movement would like us to return. I can say at this point that the eco-wiseacre who has just been elected Australian of the Year foresees an ideal population for Australia of less than a third of the number of people it has now, but he doesn't say whether he includes himself and his family among the total of those to be subtracted.

Each time I change the bins I almost subtract myself from the present total of the inhabitants of East Anglia because for evolutionary reasons I am unable to lug one bin out and push the other bin in without impacting my forehead into the top frame of the shed door.

After the first time I fell to the flagstones clutching my bisected skull, when I jokingly suggested to the three watching eco-furies that if I croaked in mid-manoeuvre they could always recycle me, I was informed that this possibility was on the cards because just outside of town there is a cemetery where they will bury you in a cardboard box.

There is also a graveyard called All Souls which has two wheelie bins standing outside it, one marked "All Souls compostable" and the other marked "All Souls non-compostable".

One of the permanent lodgers in that graveyard is the great philosopher Wittgenstein, whose key principle was that we shouldn't be seduced by language. He wanted us to say things so clearly that our meaning couldn't be mistaken. But he could only dream of that, because in fact we *are* seduced by language.

The world couldn't work if we didn't spend most of our time being open to persuasion on subjects that we will never personally investigate because we lack either the time or the talent, and usually both.

Everybody knows there are too many plastic shopping bags. You can see millions of them decorating the hedgerows. Everybody knows that it's a good sign when a supermarket puts a sign on the side of its plastic bags saying that its plastic bags are recycled from other plastic bags.

But where most of our recycled non-compostable garbage gets sorted out, hardly anybody knows. I was recently told that most of it goes to China, but I can't believe that their economic boom depends on reprocessing our tin cans, and that they won't produce rubbish of their own, and lots more of it.

There are good reasons for cleaning up the mess we make, but finally it's what we make that makes us an advanced culture, and only a highly developed industry knows how to keep itself clean.

At Bhopal in India a chemical plant once killed at least 3,800 people, but that was because it was badly regulated.

Loose supervision made it lethal. Very few nuclear reactors even in the old Soviet Union have ever gone as wrong as the one at

Chernobyl, or even the one at Three Mile Island in the US, but that's because they have regulations to meet, and the regulations themselves are the product of an industrial society.

There was a time that Japan's burgeoning post-war industry was poisoning its own people with mercury. The industry that did the poisoning found the solution, because it was forced to. But a law to suppress that industry would have helped to produce a society less able to control its own pollution, not more.

As far as I can tell with the time I've got to study the flood of information, which is less time than I would like, the green movement can do an advanced industrial society the world of good by persuading its industries to spread less poison.

Whether or not carbon emissions really do melt the polar bears and kill the baby seals in the rain forest, the pressure on industry and even on government is already helping to persuade Hollywood stars that they should drive hybrid cars, and finally we'll do what Leonardo di Caprio does, because we'll be seduced by language, not because we know very much about how carbon dioxide keeps in the planet's heat.

The other day I met a carbon dioxide expert who said that his favourite gas has already reached the density where it can't keep in any more heat, but I did notice that he was sweating.

It was probably when Sir David Attenborough noticed that the bottle-nosed dolphins were sweating that he finally gave his illustrious name to the campaign against global warming. That would be enough for me even if Prince Charles hadn't joined in as well, having already placed his order for a horse-drawn Aston Martin.

But I don't really know they're right. I'm just guessing. The only thing I do know is what won't work, because it shouldn't.

We shouldn't expect the less fortunate nations to cut themselves off from industrial progress in the name of a green planet.

It wouldn't be fair even if it was likely, and anyway, we aren't civilized by the extent to which we return to nature, only by the extent that we overcome it. I wish I'd said that. It was Sigmund Freud, actually, when they showed him the blueprints of the very first wheelie bin.

When push comes to shove, he wrote in German, this thing could still save male pride even if it can't save the planet.

PAUL MITCHELL

Contact

Did you get my email? No, where'd you send it? To your work address. I'm not on that address. Are you on your home address? Yeah, but I didn't get a message. I got your text. I didn't send a text. Yes you did. The one about your message. What message? The one you left on my work phone. Oh, but I left one later on your home phone. I didn't get that one. Have you had your mobile on? Yeah. Did you leave a message on it? No, but I sent you a text. I didn't get that text. Was it the one about your email? No, that was the one about my phone message. Which one? The one on your home phone. Oh, I only check my home messages from my work phone. Can I leave a new message on your mobile? Yeah, but don't use my work mobile. Can I text to that one? Yeah, text to it, but don't call, you can call and text to my home mobile, but remember I sometimes turn it off. Can I come to your home? Text me first to see if I'm there. Or email me. Okay, I can do that from my phone when I get to the door. It's been good talking to you. Great to catch up. Talk to you soon. Yeah, okay. Wait on … What? I'll take a picture. Can I pxt it to you later? Yeah, but not to my work mobile. I'll email it to your hotmail. Cool.

KAZ COOKE

Planet Earth: Beware of the chimps

Some stuff you just know is going to be good. Watching Amanda Vanstone block and parry Kerry O'Brien on the *7.30 Report* until he doesn't know whether to smile or scream (I wish they'd bring that back), eating at a third generation Italian restaurant, seeing a BBC natural history documentary.

The second series of BBC's *Planet Earth* is running on the ABC, and next Sunday the focus is on jungles. I don't know how much this series cost, or how many camera folk were paid for months to stake out places where no complimentary shower cap can be found (middle of the Congo, anyone?). It's so brilliant, I almost don't care how it happened.

Incidentally, I can hardly believe there was talk recently that the ABC natural history unit might be disbanded. It's one of the dumbest things I've ever heard. It feeds into history, geography, national pride, conservation, and tourism. Has anyone checked out how popular Animal Planet and similar cable stations are going, and how much product they need? Please don't leave it to Bindi Irwin's manager. If the ABC could regularly make stuff like *Planet Earth* I'd pay a licence fee and stop whingeing about that uber-amateur *Collectors* program.

Planet Earth puts the audience in a meditative state and then amazes and educates it. Accordingly, the music is sometimes a bit like the calm Enya-esque stuff piped into a salon when you get a facial, and then uses the whole drum section when the elephants heave into view. The music is all original and played by an endangered species called a real orchestra.

Even with the exquisite high-definition photography, it's hard to feel empathy with, or sympathy for the insects. Even an ant that has parasitic fungi growing out of its brain. Yeah, yeah, I know the spiders are crucial to the food chain, plus they can abseil. But euwww. It's unfair, but cute wins, especially the wide-eyed colugo, like a possum with a flying cloak—although the English call it "the flying tea-tray".

Although the quintessential narrator, David Attenborough, doesn't stomp the point, we all know that the biggest threat to all these places, and to all these creatures is us. What's climate change going to do to a place that has 2 metres of annual rainfall? Indonesia, Malaysia and Pacific islands are ripping down forests, is Papua New Guinea far behind? What about all those countries in Africa that need money and roads? Logging companies will promise both.

As we cut up the toast soldiers, knock off the tops of the boiled eggs and sit down on Sunday night to watch *Planet Earth* with our children, we can't promise them any of the stuff on this episode will still be around when they grow up. Incidentally, if you are watching with the kiddies before bedtime this Sunday, you might wish to turn it off for about five minutes after the chimp posse attacks a neighboring clan. The sight of them in victory eating the recognisable extremities of a youngster is ... let's just say, pretty indelible.

It's this scene which brings to a gibbering halt my ineluctable musings over the similarities between creatures and humans. Dominating "bully boy" capuchin monkeys could remind you of the recent Australian cricket team. The prancing, sex-craving, costume-parading birds of paradise are reminiscent of Prince on stage. A dowdy but powerful female looks a suitor over, gives him a withering glance and sweeps away. Hello, Judi Dench. Pitcher plants (LA nightclubs) lure and gobble up gangly insects (starving young social-ites). A frog in the darkness surrounded by diverse calls can hear only the warbles of its own kind (Tony Abbott). Slimy, bottom-feeding parasitic fungi; that ex-boyfriend who ... okay, this is getting kind of personal.

Thanks to this team of camera and sound folk, editors, producers—and the BBC having the money to do it—we can now "be" so close to an elephant we see every wiry hair on its crinkle parchment hide. That's why, in this episode, we see right into the eyes of those chimps, read their faces, can't dispute how similar they are to humans. Further evidence is their after-school nit check, their binge-eating of figs, and the unprovoked pre-emptive territorial attacks, right up until the "hey, you can't eat that guy's arm!" cannibal bit. They are not us. Will we protect their habitat and let them live anyway, even though they can't fund a lobbyist?

The following week, *Planet Earth* is going to take us under-water to see a flashing electric clam, sneaky sea snakes (try saying that after an eggnog), surfing dolphins, "rampaging" starfish and the "head-butting pygmy sea-horse". I don't think you can see better-crafted television than this. Not that includes headbutting, anyway.

The ABC closed its Natural History Unit in 2007 without a public announcement.

BARRY COHEN

Modern telecoms run rings around me

When she told me her name was Blackadder, I should have fled. But always the adventurer, I pressed on.

"What I require is a mobile phone. I don't want it to take photographs, tell the time, play music, provide weather forecasts or make coffee," I said. "If I can make or receive calls and record messages, that will do just fine."

"No worries," the young lady replied without sounding remotely like Rowan Atkinson. The nonsequitur should have sounded the alarm bells but the anticipation of acquiring my third mobile blinded me to reality.

The previous two had been devoured by Hamish, our border collie, who was lucky to celebrate his first birthday. As a septuagenarian I am neither digitally nor electronically literate. The mere suggestion that I should purchase some new computerised gimcrackery is enough to feel the icy claw grip my innards.

I try desperately to look interested as the saleswoman explains in great detail the wonders of the latest masterpiece of electronic gadgetry. Instead, the eyes glaze over. "This is the TU550, megapixel, three-speed, four-gear, 100-gigabyte, aerodynamic, intergalactic firkin that will change your life completely."

Unfortunately, all it will change is my blood pressure. And not for the better. Staring blankly ahead, I hand over the credit card, gather up the masterpiece and head, with what little is left of my shattered male ego, for the hills.

Arriving home I open the book of instructions, which is a mere 90 pages long in a type guaranteed to make my ophthalmologist throw a party.

The early pages are devoted to warnings: to avoid car crashes, choking children, damaging your hearing, aircraft interference or blowing yourself up by using your mobile phone near refuelling points or chemicals. After this reassuring introduction one can start learning how the device works.

A sample: "Depending on the support or not of SAT (SIM application toolkit) services on the USIM card the menu might be different. In case the USIM card supporting SAT services this menu will be the operator specific service name stored on the USIM card, for instance 'special' …" Piece of piss, really. What concerns me is that there are people who understand and are paid for writing this tosh.

I am consoled by the fact I am not alone. Our great and glorious former leader E. G. Whitlam informs me that he is not the sharpest knife in the drawer, digitally speaking.

What lunatics compose such rubbish? The least LG, Harvey Norman and Telstra should do is put you through university first.

Let me share an experience I have had on two occasions in recent years with everybody's favourite provider.

First at Calga near Gosford on the NSW central coast, and in January this year at our idyllic rural abode in Bungendore on the outskirts of the national capital, I discovered the telephone cable had been cut or broken down for some obscure reason. Our telephone was dead.

I phoned the always reliable Telstra on my trusty old mobile. In lightning time—40 minutes to be exact—I got through to

Mumbai, where I was fortunate to converse in Hinglish with my three favourite Indians: Sachin, Harbhajan and Peter Sellers.

Two phrases dominated these conversations: "excuse me" and "I beg your pardon". It apparently hasn't occurred to Telstra's supremo, the lovely, talented and extremely well-paid Sol Trujillo, that if their service personnel speak the same language as their customers, problems will be resolved much more quickly and with less angst. Maybe angst doesn't translate from English to Mexican to Hindi and back.

With great persistence I got the message through, "the line is down".

I was told "not to worry, sir, we will be transferring your calls to your mobile phone". As the alternative was to be cut off from the world for days, I agreed.

The arrival of the January bill for the mobile reminded me of my previous experience at Calga. My monthly package had increased by 30 per cent because all calls in or out were charged at the mobile rate, which, as we all know, is set by Ned Kelly.

Rather than wasting another day talking to Mumbai, getting carpal tunnel syndrome pressing buttons, and phone rage, I wrote to Telstra, the Telecommunications Ombudsman and the Minister for Communications, asking each the same simple question. "If Telstra's infrastructure goes belly-up, which will happen to the best equipment, is there any reason why I should bear the cost, rather than Telstra? If so, is it not in the interests of Telstra to have the equipment break down as often as possible?" I await with interest their response.

There are a million stories in the wonderful world of modern communications. This has been two of them.

Popular Entertainment

DAVID ASTLE

I came, I buzzed, I lost

Giddy, cotton-mouthed, I'm led down a maze of corridors with no sign of clocks or exits or daylight. I want to run. I want to pee. Famous TV people stare from the walls—comedians, chefs, weather chicks—watching me keep pace with the clipboard girl who's too busy smiling to speak. She leads me to a hallway where the names of various animals have been screwed to the doors and shunts me into the Rhino Room.

Inside, a blanket-sized mirror is framed by lightbulbs. There's a TV. Two couches. Three coathooks. "Show me your clothes," says the girl, "before you hang them up."

She scrutinises my three shirts—white, green and Hawaiian—like a paid-up member of the fashion police. "Too busy," she says of the hibiscus. "The white's too staid. Go with the green. I'll be back with the forms."

On her way out she scribbles something across the back of my door. It sounds like a texta writing my name. The cell now has its hostage.

I flick on the telly. *I Love Lucy*, circa 1957. Desi Arnaz pratfalls on a rug and slops his martini. (The canned audience laughs.) I turn down the sound and sit at the mirror, telling my reflection to relax. It's just a quiz show. It might be fun. You could win some money.

A plate of sandwiches lies at my elbow. Spam and lettuce. Spiced/ham = spam, I tell myself as a means of reminding myself I'm cluey. I know my trivia. That's why I'm here. Trapped.

The forms when they come all but gag and bind me. Like Moses skimming the commandments, I read each clause (Thou shalt not be related to production staff. Thou shalt not collude. Thou shalt not on-sell your giftshop. Thou shalt not have a heart condition) and initial them.

Make-up is down the hall and requires a chaperone to get there. Contestants are forbidden to meet face-to-face before show-time, in case empathy—and deals—are struck. My escort, another clipboard girl, introduces herself as B2.

"After the banana?" I banter, banally. My cocktail charms have fled. My power of speech has fled. All traces of intelligence have fled.

"Belinda's the coordinator," she deadpans. "I'm the second Belinda."

My hair has undesirable wings, the coiffeur tells me. Wings are bad in studio light. I need "product" to tamp things down. Again that blank buffoon gazes back from the mirror, posing the question:

For a pick of the board, who am I? Born in 1961, the eldest son of a loving bourgeois family that had no desire to invite humiliation to its home, he went on to flop in *Sale of the Century* in 1981, and later *Jeopardy*, winning nought but embarrassment for his troubles. Not only did he forget where Angel Falls fell, or who put pussy in the well, but the same bloke omitted the "o" from diarrhoea on national television. To prove he's a slow learner, he's now competing in a gameshow that trades on impotence and disgrace. I am …

Fact is, I am a lot of Australians. As gameshow fodder we share a history of heartbreaks. Why do we do it? Why do we embark on such flights of lunacy and greed, where tears and fears and ignominy are waiting at the other end?

Scan the telly guide and you'll see how pandemic the plague has become. Once upon a time Barry Jones picked-a-box, or Barbie Rogers embodied the *Great Temptation*, but now the dam has burst. Citizens have every chance to play the patsy in *Deal or No Deal, Rich List, RocKwiz, Are You Smarter than a 5th Grader?, Wipeout, Gladiators, Con Test, Family Feud, The New Price Is Right, The New Wheel of Fortune, 1 vs 100, Hole in the Wall* and *The Einstein Factor,* leaving aside the mania of radio competitions, funny home videos and frenzied post-school quizzes for kids. We buy a vowel, risk snakebite, snog on camera, propose on camera, disappear through trapdoors, sweat to heartbeat music, stab colleagues in the back and risk the national debt of Argentina—for what?

If money was your answer, deduct $5. Because winning money, or a full-length Drizabone with interior stitching, is just a sliver of the gameshow story.

Greed is a primary human motivator, right up there with libido and revenge, but you can't tell me a thousand Australians every year spin fortune's wheel, catch Burgo's phrase and walk the walk of shame purely for the one-off shot of scoring a shekel. Okay, maybe half do. (Deduct $2.50.) But what else prompts such pathological behaviour? Why do so many ostensibly sensible people risk face-loss in the national loungeroom?

"I look at it in terms of playacting," says Heather Cameron-Grey, a Melbourne psychologist who specialises in humiliation. "Because playacting is not a life-or-death situation, it can carry the sense we're invincible. I also think it's the fantasy of 'getting away with it', like doing something 'naughty', making love on the beach or something. People aren't aware of the real consequences."

I'm too scared to ask, but I can't help myself. Consequences like what?

"Shame," says Cameron-Grey, "which is very scarring. People don't realise the psychological damage. Because shame is based on memory, we replay it."

But wait. Surely the buzz of taking part inoculates you against eventual blows of the being out-buzzed?

Cameron Grey can't agree. "When excitement is cut short so quickly, we're left with a high level of neural firing, a wash of chemicals which causes a heating in the face. In the face we get that caved-in look."

Not my face. I'm pancaked, invincible and my wings are gelled down.

~

Back in 1981, so keen was I to be mocked by Tony Barber, I played dumb with the producers on *Sale of the Century*. To quote Rocky Rhodes, the non-flying rooster on *Chicken Run*, "I didn't lie Dollface, I omitted certain truths."

The truth was this: B1's counterpart back in 1981 phoned me a week before the recording. She asked if everything was fine for the trip to Melbourne. Sure, I said, forgetting to mention I had 26 brand-new stitches around my left eye from copping a rugby boot at close quarters. Twice. The wound was grotesque, a no-no for family dinnertime viewing, but that's the irrational desire I'm meaning, the fantasy, the crazed urge to gamble with the ego.

(Channel 9 beauticians spent an hour trying to camouflage the welts and mercurochrome, all for me to forget where Angel Falls fell—and fall. Yes, I still have the stickpin.)

Face fixed, I walk back to the Rhino Room, a traipse down Death Row with my snake-hipped jailer in tow, and hear the cell door shut behind me. I feel like sobbing. Escaping. Not for the first time I realise that the gameshow system is Woomera with sandwiches. You lose all status, all claims to civility. Prodded into chutes like so many milkers, you enter a subclass devoid of grace and surnames, a succession of wannabes who squint into Camera 3 when the red light flicks on. Meantime the paperwork, the dotted lines, the box-ticking cancels your last hope of being an individual. Clauses 1–22 as good as sew your lips.

Which may explain the secret scars among our neighbours. For all we know, every second ratepayer around us has undergone their own public putdown in half-hour slots, but the pre-show contracts swear our muteness afterwards. There is no victim support, no sob circle among the runners-up. Legally, we cannot divulge our trauma. (When this story first ran I had to rely on the pseudonym of Steve Bennett, the pet alias of Bart Simpson, to blow the whistle.) Worse than football injuries, the gameshow experience doesn't respond to suturing or iodine. It cannot be seen. Nor spoken of.

Little Johnny Green put pussy in the well, I say, and Morgan Freeman drove Miss Daisy. Just relax. Chill out. Have a sandwich. Watch Lucy.

I'm not a timid person. Zoologists might label me as an alpha male. Tallish, a firm handshake, polished shoes, a grab-bag of credible opinions, I can string a few words together. But put me under lights and ask me what arachnophobes fear and I'm likely to say Copenhagen.

The door opens. I have an inmate, a rat-spunky waiter called Tony. B1 helps him pick a shirt, tells him moccasins are too déclassé, and shuts the door.

Tony is booked for the episode after mine. Hence we can talk, assuming I won't be the carry-over champion, which is a fair assumption. We talk about tactics, and alienation, and the one-day cricket which we locate on the television. A Kiwi gets bowled first ball and slumps back to the pavilion with a weeping duck under his ribcage—the original walk of shame. TV has a long and rich history of degradation.

"So why do we do it?" I ask Tony.

My cellmate aspires to being a guinea pig on Channel 9's *Fear Factor*, the latest series of macho brinkmanship, a sort of *Gladiators* meets *Who Dares Wins* with a teaspoonful of *Survivor*, and maybe going on this "quiz thing" will help boost his chances. Like I say, jackpots and giftshops are just a smokescreen.

B1 is back again. "We're doing a walk-through in five," she tells me. "Check out the set. Test the electricals."

"Any chance of using the toilet?"

She frowns. Looks at her watch. "I'll have to go with you."

Under my breath, walking past the other private rooms, seeing my competitors' names written on the doors and wishing I was elsewhere, I spell diarrhoea with an "o".

~

Months before this gruelling day of Nivea and trivia were the auditions, fifty general knowledge questions in a disused studio, followed by a "personality" form that asked such zingers as:

- You have five minutes left to live. What will you do?
- Name a law that should be abolished.
- You and a friend are sitting in the bar of a five-star hotel, when you find a Rolex watch on the adjacent table. Do you tell your friend? Keep it? Hand it in?

In the column reserved for personal hobbies/interests, I made light of the truth. What's the point of putting down the obvious? To debase yourself properly, you need to err on the side of zany, claiming such pursuits as kite-surfing and fingerprinting in order to catch the producer's eye. At the *Jeopardy* audition, on paper at least, I boomeranged and ate fire. Only to be thrashed, come the hour, by a bilingual greenkeeper from Mona Vale.

A friend of mine, Becky, said her house was haunted for the sake of scoring a gig on the Roy/HG gameshow back in 2000. The ploy did the trick at auditions, only for Messrs Slaven and Nelson to spend half the episode grilling my mate on the ghost's personal hygiene habits and choice of TV shows. Even before the gameshow concludes, the contestant knows that caved-in feeling.

Over and over. Like a custard-wearing clown who clean forgets the latest salvo of pies, I stand at my module awaiting the cameras to roll. With three gameshows behind me, am I an optimist, a masochist, a fatalist or recidivist? Or (e), all of the above.

"One of the wonderful things about human nature," reckons Cameron-Grey, "is that we want to resolve the past. An example is people who continually go into marriages which are similar, and have similar outcomes. It stems from a wish to resolve the initial sense of failure, of going back into the same situation."

Quizzes or marriages—seems the psyche is trapped in a win/loss spool. "[Repeat behaviour] comes from a desire to heal, to conquer, to come out the winner, so that the future won't have that [negative] pattern."

Spotlights swivel. An army of floor staff futz around with gaffer tape and light meters, barking into Britney-like headsets and monkeying up scaffolding. I notice one dude has a T-shirt saying "9 days, 24 surfers, 21 stops, 1 bus" and wonder if that's the sort of thing a focused contestant ought be noticing on the eve of triumph.

Just before the signature tune revs up, my fellow contestants have a chance to trade grimaces, and whisper "good luck" to each other. That's the thing, we understand suffering. We don't despise our fellow lab rat, despite the animosity that oozes from the home screen. It's just a game.

Though Cameron-Grey sees something different. "Viewers identify with the host—the abuser—and the winner—who is the strongest, the survivor. Gameshows once had consolation prizes for the runners-up, board games and stickpins, because they used to play fair. But now fair isn't entertaining."

Gagged and bound, I'm not at liberty to identify the host, or the protocol, or the bastard who beat me because he knew Paul Keating managed a rock-n-roll combo called The Ramrods in the sixties, which I knew too, but the buzzer deals in nanoseconds, hence everyone at home, including my peers who once took me for intelligent, think I'm an idiot. And I am. Correct. You win $22,000.

Our show's winner, through a blend of brains and deceit, bags that sort of cash, and nobody feels happy about it, not even the host or the winner herself. She skulks about the backroom corridor after the show, looking sheepish in a lurex blouse, and apologises to the runner-up who naturally enough won nothing.

"I feel terrible," she says to her gypped rival. "If I had my time over ... I guess at the end of the day it's just a game."

Given her chance, the runner-up would kill the winner. She'd eat the winner's liver with fava beans and a nice Chianti. Instead she shrugs, begrudges a smile and looks for the nearest exit. The bitterness is palpable, everyone too raw and ravaged and wrung out for tears or gentle sincerities. It's a brutality we call entertainment. Where Roman society threw slaves into tiger clashes and mock sea-battles, we cast our own frail selves into freak attritions that go by the name of gameshows.

I go home heavy-hearted, empty-handed. My so-called reward from the four-hour torment is a spam and lettuce sandwich, plus the chance to watch my lowest half-hour on the box. But I renege, once the timeslot comes. I don't need to go there. I have the shame already and, like a video souvenir, I replay it every day.

IAN CUTHBERTSON

You just know it will be deliciously messy

"Why are you so quiet?" Lena (Emily Rose) asks Justin (Dave Annable), in the afterglow of the lovemaking session they both decided should not happen in the previous episode of *Brothers & Sisters*. Why not? Well, Justin had developed an addiction to painkillers, was in recovery from it, was not ready for a commitment (apparently sex is the kind of pleasure that's a no-no for recovering addicts; perhaps they will replace their substance abuse with sex addiction or something), and he was already late for a meeting with his sponsor. "Ah, screw it," he had said, somewhat indelicately I thought, before locking lips with luscious Lena.

Lena, you see, works at the wine-producing offshoot of the Walker family business. She's been having it off with handsome Tommy Walker (Balthazar Getty) since his adored wife went home to mommy, blaming him for the death of one of their twins, a decision they made together, as viewers would recall.

But wifey has come to her senses and Lena has shifted to troubled, recovering addict and war-injured Justin. So far, so soapy, you think? Well, to a point.

The terrific thing about *B&S* is that we know more about the characters' lives than they do. Justin doesn't know Lena has been diddling his brother. And Tommy doesn't know she is diddling Justin.

This sense of being ahead of the revelations for the characters leads to some juicy ironies, most uncommon in American soaps, er, dramas.

It works best with the queen of adultery, still the series' most interesting character, Holly Harper (Patricia Wettig), who works with Tommy in the Walker wine business.

Holly bore Walker patriarch William an illegitimate child, Rebecca, who strives to integrate herself, as a legitimate half-sister, into the already outsized Walker clan.

Lena works with Holly and Tommy, so the knowingness that viewers share with Holly, who sees all between Lena, Tommy and Tommy's wife Julia (Sarah Jane Morris), is delicious.

Brothers & Sisters is at its best when it strives to integrate unusual elements into the Walker clan (and the show), such as adultery and its consequences, through the generations, and the troubled sexual and romantic life of gay Walker brother Kevin, played with terrific wit and sure-footed self-confidence by Matthew Rhys.

It's at its worst when it falls into quirky urban neuroticism, which seems to be the strong suit of mother Nora (Sally Field) and sister Kitty (Calista Flockhart). Tonight there's way too much of the latter as Kitty and senator Robert McCallister (Rob Lowe) tie the knot. You'll wonder if you haven't flicked back in time to Flockhart as that notorious queen of quirk, Ally McBeal.

LARISSA DUBECKI

Madonna's latest offering leaves listener pondering: Just because she can, does it mean she should?

Say what you will about Madonna's music; she continues to be a master—or perhaps that should be mistress—semiotician from the Benny Hill school of innuendo.

The title of her latest album, *Hard Candy*, refers to both her yoga-buffed body and the self-belief that she remains a scorching sexual proposition, a stance furthered by the lyrics to the single "Candy Shop": "I'll be your one stop/ candy store/ lollipop/ have some more/ my sugar is raw/ sticky and sweet."

Clearly, the near-saturation level of global recognition she enjoys is not based on her wit, but Madonna has other claims to fame. Few other 49-year-old women, for example, would consider wearing an album cover outfit consisting of little more than a black swimsuit, thigh-high leather boots and an ecstatic expression.

Fewer still could boast a career spanning 26 years, or that each new album release is a keenly anticipated event—although her status is based less on the quality of her musical output and more on her infamous talent for reinvention.

She has gone from the rebellious Catholic schoolgirl of *Like a Virgin* to cowgirl (*Music*), urban guerilla (*American Life*) and purple-leotard-wearing disco princess (*Confessions on a Dancefloor*).

Hard Candy, her 11th album of original material, which is released in Australia today, doesn't disappoint on that count. Hip hop–influenced R&B is the flavour du jour. Corralled for the project were Justin Timberlake, who co-wrote five of the songs and sings on four, plus top-shelf R&B producers Pharrell Williams and Timbaland.

As the world's highest-selling female recording artist told this month's *Vanity Fair* of working with the hottest songwriters and producers: "I needed to be inspired and thought, well, who's making records I like? So I went, I like that guy and I like that guy."

The Material Girl's music is in many ways immaterial to her career, but with the artist turning 50 in August, *Hard Candy* is in many ways a stab at ongoing relevance, despite her quite believable promise that "I can go on and on", on a track called "Heartbeat".

The trouble is that, while her longevity has been based on an almost uncanny ability to plunder subcultures and turn them into mainstream trends, *Hard Candy* comes across as a thinly veiled attempt to keep up with an already forward-thinking pack of R&B-flavoured artists including Gwen Stefani, Christina Aguilera and Nelly Furtado.

It is unlikely to tempt the thirtysomethings who pester wedding DJs to play "Into the Groove". Nor is it going to impress children who associate Madonna with their parents' vinyl collection, despite "Four Minutes to Save the World" giving the impression she threatened Timberlake with an electric cattle prod left over from the "American Life" video to repeat her name over an insistent beat.

Elsewhere, Kanye West pops in for a spot of self-aggrandising rapping on "Beat Goes On", while Madonna shares her insights about how you don't have to be rich and famous to be good ("Dance 2Nite"), and, in "Incredible", we discover how great her husband, British film director Guy Ritchie, is in the sack ("Sex with you is incredible … metaphysical," she warbles).

Hard Candy is no answer to the retro-disco pop of 2005's *Confessions on a Dancefloor*.

Those who fail to find any relevance in the Madonna juggernaut may be left posing this question about the desperation faintly perfuming her *Hard Candy* Gucci-does-dominatrix image, and her latter-day music: Just because she can, does it mean she should?

MARIEKE HARDY

A time to repent: *Big Brother*'s over

So the comely goons have packed away their wee bathing costumes and mystifying array of headwear for the year and the Gold Coast compound has been disinfected and bulldozed or whatever it is that happens to the *Big Brother* house once its dizzy half-dressed residents stumble into the wider world.

And those of us who have bothered to catch more than one episode of the series can finally relax/repent. Bless me Father, for I have sat through *BB* 2007 in its entirety and, try as I might, I can't seem to wash the blood from my hands.

For all its hinted at glamour, its conveyor belt of grinning wholewheat dill pickles, its comfortingly inane tasks, the '07 series just didn't sparkle. Even Mama Killeen was looking tired and irritable this year, presumably biting the heads off a few bats backstage before prowling out to ensnare a hapless halfwit in her verbal net and relieve them of their lifeblood.

Watching to see which terrified assistant slipped up with their autocue work each week and faced the poisonous glare from her laser eyes (I'm convinced she sleeps upside down or in some kind of futuristic ice chamber) was a mild diversion from the weekly tedium of feigning excitement over evictions, but not enough.

Everyone involved with the show seemed bored by the concept, the routines. How were the rest of us simple-minded fools supposed to get on board for our dose of cheesecore television when our hosts couldn't even bother getting off the couch to greet us?

"What *Big Brother* promises, he delivers," we were told via thundering voice-over in the weeks preceding lift-off. If a subdued mob of dullards treading water for 100 days and barely mustering the energy for a few limp rounds of Marco Polo in the pool was one of the original items on the "must have" agenda, then *BB* has certainly come through with the goods.

Whether the disappointingly tepid choice of housemates was simply a reaction to last year's Turkey Slap incident (there was something privately enjoyable about watching Helen Coonan repeatedly use those words in Parliament, wasn't there?) or—frighteningly—Australia has just milked its supply of ambitious dumbbells dry, the show failed to produce a character who set us alight. Where was our defiant Merlin, our adorably thick Reggie, our politically dynamic (swoon) Lefty Tim?

Last Monday's Final Eviction Cashback Bonanza Johnny Casino Goodtimes was memorable mostly for the fact that it went about 18 years over schedule and several of the housemates waiting to be interviewed by *Big Brother* crossed over into middle age during the course of the program.

A limp, drawn-out affair that proved a sadly fitting climax for a series that failed to set the nation's texting teens on fire, it ambled from forgettable one-on-ones with friends and family members, to some of the most awkward time-filling since Molly Meldrum desperately attempted to subdue a rather refreshed Iggy Pop on *Countdown*.

Let's face it, when even knuckle-dragging truckie Travis cottons on that the producers have run out of material and are informing their host to just "tread water", you ain't fooling anybody.

Vox pops with the crowd fared little better—there's only so many times you can watch Mr Gold Coast Mike Goldman lean into a terrified-looking child and ask them who they think will win before you become sorely tempted to go do rum shooters at the pub instead.

Monday's other two standout moments involved Gretel being hit in the head by a rubber chicken thrown by a toothsomely imbecilic ninny named Bodie (police are yet to find his remains, though judging from the murderous expression on Killeen's face post-collision there wouldn't have been much left for the crows to pick over) and a cheerily half-baked pantomime performed by the housemates that was so utterly horrifying I have written a strongly worded letter to my local MP demanding all involved be lined up and shot.

From what I witnessed through my self-imposed finger jail, the piece was supposed to be some kind of cheeky, self-reverential knees-up romp but in actuality was more excruciatingly embarrassing than having a naked sauna with your uncle.

Anyway, in the long run, I know, I know … you're right—it's *Big Brother*.

Me sitting here complaining about the lack of sexy zing in this particular reality television show is like turning up at Mardi Gras and musing aloud that there seem to be rather a lot of homosexuals in attendance. You know what you're signing up for when you throw yourself at the mercy of Gretel and co.

I only hope that next year they manage to relocate their mojo and give us sinners something worth repenting for.

MARIEKE HARDY

Lashings of lust curved up by Nigella

I get the sneaking suspicion—and I'm quite happy to be proven wrong here—that a large portion of the sisterhood isn't all that keen on Nigella Lawson. We like food, certainly. Some of us are also partial to boobies, and innuendo, and ladies with big, round bottoms, but even then Nigella seems to make selected members of the wymmyn's network slightly suspicious.

Perhaps it's the chocolatey vowels and habit of rolling herself all over the preparation space in a fashion that would be considered deeply unhygienic by most food and safety officers. Perhaps it's the overly posh "grahnd piahno and plahstic bahgs" business. It could even be the high-waisted trou. Most of all, though, I'm guessing what many folk get their knickers slightly twisted about is the heavy lashings of sauce. And I'm not referring to the lady's condiments pantry.

The unadulterated in-your-face smorgasbord of sexuality—for let us not pretend for a moment *Nigella Feasts* is anything but—is on display from the opening credits. A pair of lusty red animated lips opens up and makes good work of a glistening cherry. A curvaceous lemon is lustily sliced in two. A line of asparagus spears stand firm and erect, presumably awaiting a thorough blanching.

There's absolutely no escaping the orgiastic celebration of pulsating lust. Even in moments of idle chitchat Nigella sounds as though she's moments away from opening the door to a team of rowdy sailors looking for rumpo and giving them a full oil and lube. "I find it really … *hard* …" she breathes, gazing longingly into the lens, before throwing in as an almost whispered verbal postscript, "… to zest citrus fruit". "OOOOH, JUICY JUICY!" she climaxes later still, when a wayward lime threatens to drench the camera crew with its pulpy innards. By the time she gets elbow-deep into kneading some raw lamb mince you'll be forced to cover the eyes of your children and lead them from the room with firm instructions to go directly to bed with a cold wash cloth. Why Nigella doesn't just cut out the middleman and strip naked while pounding the mince into submission with her buttocks is beyond me. At the very least it would lay down a not uninteresting gauntlet to Kylie Kwong.

Anyway, all that innuendo and trite "tee hee, we're so naughty in the kitchen together" business shouldn't work, it really shouldn't. It's too needy; too in-your-face and wanting to be fondled, like your year 11 art teacher who perhaps shouldn't be let loose around teenage boys after one too many rum babas at the school formal. Who among us not attending Sex Addicts Anonymous actually describes yoghurt as "voluptuous", or employs the idiotic term "stir as if you meant it"? I wanted to write Lawson off as an oversexed dandy with a bitching shelf and leave her to her sticky, dollybird kitchen and seductively shiny accoutrements. I wanted to denounce the lame celebrity chef phenomenon and turn my back on school marm-ly British femmes with wealthy husbands and a penchant for nosh. But I couldn't.

Oh lordy, I submitted. Completely. Before 10 minutes had passed in last week's Lebanese feasting episode, I was helplessly drawn in. By all of it. Her sharp, delectable nose, the way she fondled her aubergine. I've never wanted to be a portion of aubergine so much in my life, not counting the time I accidentally swallowed a tablet of dishwashing powder and thought my name was Vanguard the Invincible for three days. Nigella's perfect pink fingers, and the way she picked at pinenuts, or sifted "fat flakes of salt", absolutely did my head in. By the time she took her perky woven basket and strode off to the market to buy pistachios I was ready to chase her along the street and climb on for a patootie ride like Robert Crumb. She simply reduces the viewer to the most base of emotions—lust, hunger, the urge to take a sizeable bite from her backside. I have no idea how. I can't cook to save my life and have absolutely no interest in learning, and even still I plan to tune in to *Nigella Feasts* until the day I die.

It's just that she's so deliciously *plummy*. The cool, collected kitchen, the blush of peachy V at her decolletage, the milky British sunlight setting her wicked self aglow as she artfully creates gastronomic warfare. She's prim and proper and "let's all have a jolly nice afternoon playing hockey" while simultaneously undressing celery sticks with her eyes. It's like being tied up with leather straps and flogged by Enid Blyton.

So forgive me for capitulating to what is essentially a cheap grab at the audience groin. I'm base and repulsive, I know. The question begs asking, though—if the *Nigella Feasts* producers are going to push this panting, licky-licky she-beast upon us in such blatantly rabid style, why not go the whole hog and dress her in a pair of polka-dot knickers and sequinned nipple tassels? I'd tape every episode.

God, she's fantastically obscene. Someone come and hose me down; I'm on fire like Bruce Springsteen self-immolating.

GARRY WILLIAMS

Interview with Ja'mie King

It's been a big year at Summer Heights High for Ja'mie King—
but that doesn't mean she can't wait to leave the povvos behind
again …

Q: How has the Summer Heights High experience been for you?
A: When I look back at what I've achieved I'm SO blown away.
Making friends with the hottest girls in year 11, getting a year 7
boyfriend, dumping him, being President of the SRC, the fashion
parade, formal, going out with a lesbian. It's been an incredible
experience. The whole school is going to be SO lost without me.

Q: Do you feel pressure to look hot all the time?
A: I have natural hotness so I don't feel pressure because I'm basically
what I call "Born Hot".

Q: Why did you pick this dress?
A: It was designed to show off my assets: arse, legs and face and
enhance my boobs and make them appear bigger than they really
are. I looked into getting breast implants for the formal, but there's
a six-week recovery period so I couldn't.

Q: Do you have your eating disorder under control?
A: Yes. I only starve for events now. Like dates, formals, school photos. Two or three days without food prior to an event can totally improve skin and body tone.

Q: Going to the formal with a lesbian when you're straight sends a message of acceptance. Was that the intention?
A: Not really. It was more the shock factor. And lesbians are really in at the moment and I always like to be on top of fashion and trends.

Q: Do you see yourself as a role model for teenagers?
A: People always say I am and I can see why. It's so random, but I've got this secret dream that all teenage girls in the world become just like me. It would be an amazing world, wouldn't it?

Q: The girls at SHH seemed to worship you. Why was that?
A: I think public school girls are always fascinated by private school ones. It's like if you drove a crap car and like a Rolls-Royce parked next to you. You would totally want to check it out.

Q: Are you going to miss SHH?
A: As if. I don't want to be a bitch, but why would I miss sitting in a fibro classroom with a bunch of skanks and no airconditioning listening to a teacher who was too crap to get a job at a private school? Seriously.

ANDREW HANSEN, DOMINIC KNIGHT,
CHAS LICCIARDELLO, JULIAN MORROW
AND CRAIG REUCASSEL

The Chaser's Logies

We've been asked to help Channel Nine make the Logies into a high-quality, entertaining, watchable TV show.

An impossible task, but we're gonna try.

And to be fair, it's not that Nine's people are incapable of doing things well—it's just that they usually wait until they're working for Seven to start doing it.

For that reason, the first way we'd help out Nine is by simply moving the whole Logies show to Seven. After all, the basic idea of any commercial program is to take a hackneyed format with mediocre performers and miraculously turn it into a giant money-making success. David Leckie's done that with *Gladiators*, so surely he's the man to do it for the Logies.

The telecast

When it comes to making the Logies night telecast enjoyable for people at home, we're looking overseas for inspiration—to awards telecasts such as the Emmys and the BAFTAs. And we realised the Logies would be far more popular if they combined the best thing about American TV awards (i.e. Eddie McGuire does not appear) and the best thing about British TV awards (i.e. they're simply not televised in this country).

But if we really must broadcast the Logies here, we have no choice but to spice things up by borrowing techniques from other, more popular shows. Taking our lead from *Gladiators*, we'll make everyone wear a lycra bodysuit—including John Wood. Viewers will be delighted to know we're also being inspired by *Underbelly*, and murdering 35 people before the show is over. Finally, we will showcase the personal side of the ceremony by filming an adaptation of *I'm a Celebrity … Get Me Out of Here!*, entitled *I'm a Celebrity … Get Me a Line of Coke*.

The red carpet

To improve the broadcast, Nine needs to use its stable of talent better. Why have Richard Wilkins turning the red carpet beige when Nine could deploy news boss John Westacott to assess the f—ability of starlets? Any disagreements about Westacott's assessments will be settled in the usual way—with Supreme Court evidence that Nine tries to suppress and Crikey publishes.

The pre-Logies red carpet is always so dreary, but remember it is red. All it would take to turn this part of the night into must-watch TV is one half-starved bull. Watching an enraged steer flattening Matthew Newton will be far more amusing than asking him what he's wearing. (And would provide a bit of revenge for Brooke Satchwell.)

The host

The host needs to be someone who really understands boozy, drug-fuelled evenings—Wayne Carey. He can follow up the Logies by appearing on *Enough Rope* and denying they ever happened.

Guest presenters

"Here's an idea. How 'bout we get two stars together who don't know each other, give them an awkwardly written unfunny script, make sure they don't attend a rehearsal, and then get them to stumble through it live on air before making a lame segue to the award they are giving."

These were the words of James Oscar in 1923, which revolutionised the awards ceremony format and are still used today as the blueprint for ceremonies such as the Logies.

What few realised is that James Oscar then uttered in late 1924: "Oh, that doesn't work, please make them stop." Unfortunately he was ignored. It is time we listened to him.

Problem is, dispensing with the awkward banter script only makes things worse, because actors are all such boring individuals when playing themselves. The only viable solution is to appoint Chris Lilley to play every single presenter and co-presenter. Since this would make it difficult for Chris to also appear as himself (rightfully winning every category he's been nominated in) we'll get John Clarke to play Lilley when receiving his awards.

Awards and punishments

One of the major problems with the Logies is that it is only a "celebration" of Australian TV. This needs to be balanced by some castigation of those shows and stars who need to be punished and discouraged. Daryl Somers' drive to return to television, for example, has been fuelled by the row of Gold Logies lining his living room shelves. If there were a few well-deserved Golden Turds on his shelves then maybe his return would be less swift and therefore a mercy to us all.

In Norway the equivalent of the Logies, De Brunershulderfelts, effectively incorporates the carrot-and-stick approach by lashing the makers of awful TV with frozen herrings and then throwing them briefly in an ice hole. As a result, poor programming has significantly decreased there while ratings for the awards ceremony are at an all-time high. Here, if the producers of *The Resort* and *Let Loose Live* had been thrown to crocodiles during previous Logies, then we wouldn't have been subjected to *Monster House* this year.

In fact, forget the old Logies rules. Time for some rules people can relate to—schoolyard rules. Most Popular Entertainer gets to pash a looker. Least Popular gets a wedgie. And viewers would certainly tune in to watch the entire cast of *Quizmania* getting their heads flushed in toilets.

We'd also like to introduce one brand-new category, the Where Are They Now? award. This will comprise soapie actors reaccepting awards they won five years ago—only now, the actors must wear their waiter's aprons while receiving the trophy.

Acceptance speeches

Each year threats are made by the organisers about winners making overly lengthy speeches. But so far they are not heeded. The Oscars approach of retracting the microphone was the most effective method, although even then it left bent-over stars thanking God into the hole in the lectern. We have a solution. If celebrities insist on giving acceptance speeches, then they will only be allowed to give a single web address where interested viewers can go to read the hundreds of names that the starlets would like to thank. This will cut the duration of the telecast by about seven hours. On their website, the celebs can also express their "complete surprise" at winning.

Ultimately, though, we've decided to forbid any actual celebrities from giving speeches at all. It works like this. Despite the fact that most Logies attendees manage to escape the horror of the show and spend the whole night outside the ballroom, the seats are amazingly never empty in the camera wide shots. This is thanks to Nine's army of "seat warmers"—extras who are hired to sit in empty seats so the room appears full to home viewers. Last year at the Logies, one member of *The Chaser* actually found himself at a table of these well-dressed extras and not a single genuine guest. Not only were the seat warmers better dressed anyway, they were far more interesting to talk to—which is why all acceptance speeches ought be given by the seat warmers.

Cameras everywhere

Part of the dullness of Logies telecasts is that the cameras are trained on the most boring part of the night—the awards ceremony. We would like viewers to be given access to Bar-Cam so they can see the real highlight: the US guest star (this is usually someone relatively obscure, like Dennis Haysbert, and the fact that you haven't heard of him only proves the point—he was the President from *24*) trying to get into the pants of the nearest well-endowed publicist.

Recent Logies have featured live crosses to a smaller room outside for unguarded interviews with the winners. They should cross to an even smaller room where celebrities are far more unguarded— the toilet. There we can witness the Best New Talent still clasping her freshly won trophy while yocking up her complimentary Vodka Cruisers.

Because the Logies take place in Crown Casino, another avenue is for the telecast to be fed from the security cameras in the pokies room downstairs. Slowly watching a grandmother fritter away her pension will be much more cheerful than the normal ceremony, and you may even catch the odd kneecapping from a stand-over man. In fact, for viewers in Victoria this may be the closest they get to seeing *Underbelly* this year.

In memoriam

Rather than showing "In Memoriam" packages for deceased people no one has heard of, we would like tribute to be paid to the far more tragic deaths of TV shows such as *The Power of 10*, *Yasmin's Getting Married*, and whatever show Nine gets Bert Newton to host this year.

Guest singer

The Logies feature performances by visiting musical guests from overseas, but in an era when all our own TV personalities are willing to sing on *It Takes Two*, this seems an unnecessary waste of a galaxy of home-grown stars. Rather than being forced to watch Avril Lavigne lip-syncing her latest pap, viewers will instead watch Sandra Sully performing Britney Spears' *Toxic* and *Gardening Australia*'s Peter Cundall crooning Justin Timberlake's *SexyBack*. We'll take anyone—the only rule being that under no circumstances will Daryl Somers be allowed to sing. In fact, we'll have the security personnel prevent him from entering the room at all.

Voting

We could make the Logies score a profit for the first time in history. If Nine really wants people to vote by SMS, they should give them an incentive: every voter who sends an SMS will receive an annoying ringtone and a picture of a horny Russian babe.

Yes, giving out a public number for people to text is risky, so an entire call centre will be set up specifically to deal with the thousands of dirty messages the nominees will receive from Shane Warne.

Furthermore, all the prizes will be announced using the *Up Late Game Show* method. The winners' names will be used as obvious clues in a guessing game for home viewers—so for the Gold, it might be KATE R-TCHIE. The drawback of this is that the Logies will have to be hosted by Hotdogs. Sorry.

Charity

Some nasty cynics describe the Logies as a shallow orgy of money-grubbing self-congratulation. We need to find a way to divert attention from the fact that those people are right. The best way to do that is to link Logies night with a good cause. In particular, the Logies should get on the climate change bandwagon by teaming up with Earth Hour—a 60-minute blackout during the middle of the ceremony would be a considerable improvement. Everyone would feel better about themselves, not just because they'd be helping to save the planet, but also because they wouldn't have to watch those dreadful award categories SBS always wins like Most Outstanding Public Affairs Report.

But an Earth Hour tie-in would only be the start of an environmental initiative. To really eliminate noxious emissions, we'll also ensure Kyle Sandilands isn't invited.

The after party

Everyone knows (or at least suspects) the real entertainment at the Logies happens at the after parties. To ensure that this year's event goes off like no other, we'll appoint Corey Worthington as the official host—on the condition Max Markson doesn't get a cut. We'll invite everyone except for *A Current Affair* summer host Leila McKinnon, who'll be forced to gatecrash with her fella, Nine chief executive David Gyngell.

The Arts

SHANE MALONEY

Cook's tour: Peter Cook

If Peter Cook hasn't done much in the past 12 years, that's only because he's dead. Before then, he did quite a bit—although the obituaries tended to infer that he had squandered his prodigious talent. Since that talent consisted essentially of being the funniest man in the world, it is difficult to imagine how he might better have expended it than pottering around, smacking the occasional golf ball, pretending to be a Norwegian fisherman, having a few drinks and leaving ever-expanding ripples of laughter in his wake.

In 1987, his rigorous gift-frittering regime brought him to Australia as guest of honour of the inaugural Melbourne International Comedy Festival. Far too unpredictable to be allowed out on his own, he was allocated a minder. That task fell to me. It was the best job I've ever had.

For the previous three years, I'd been employed by Melbourne City Council to run its cultural program. This consisted mainly of wangling free concert tickets for the councillors. Elton John, if possible. The opera, if there was nothing else up for grabs.

The allure of this task had begun to wear thin. I was ready to jump ship. And when a rag-tag collection of small-time theatre promoters knocked on the town hall door, jester's cap in hand, asking the council to bankroll their plans for a comedy festival, I saw my chance.

From Barry Humphries onward, Melbourne has long been a fertile breeding ground for comedy. By the mid-'80s, comedy venues were springing up all over town, television was tapping into the talent and even the city fathers wanted a piece of the action.

They weren't too sure, however, about handing a bucket of cash to a bunch of shady-looking joke-brokers. I suggested that instead of money, they be given in-kind support. To wit, a council officer on secondment. Somebody to see that the jokes ran on time, that the books were kept in good order and that dodgy promoters didn't abscond with the takings. Somebody like me, say.

The councillors bought it. Lock, stock and whoopee cushion.

John Pinder, proprietor of the Last Laugh and the Sydney Greenstreet of Melbourne comedy, took me under his voluminous wing and we set to work to hammer out a program. *The Age* agreed to run a spoof front cover on our launch date, April Fool's Day. The chief magistrate volunteered his court as the venue for a mock trial. A trio of young actors of ethnic persuasion put together a show called *Wogs Out of Work*. Marching girls were booked and Wendy Harmer was put on sedatives.

The only thing missing was a marquee attraction. A comedic luminary of global proportions, a name so big that even journalists would recognise it. Peter Cook, for example. Assuming, of course, that he wasn't too busy pulling lobsters out of Jayne Mansfield's bottom or teaching ravens to fly underwater.

Cook had a longstanding connection with Australia. In 1971, he and Dudley Moore toured here for nearly five months, test-driving *Behind the Fridge* before its premiere in the West End. Australia loved Pete and Dud, revelling in their irreverence and surreal wordplay. The tour was a triumph, the shows were sold out and the media couldn't get enough of them. Several weeks into the run, they performed a sketch on the *Dave Allen Show* on the Nine Network. Called "The

Gospel Truth", it took the form of an interview by Bethlehem Star reporter Matthew (Dudley) of Mr Arthur Shepherd (Pete).

The skit created an immediate furore. Hundreds of irate viewers besieged the switchboard with complaints and the Australian Broadcasting Control Board immediately banned the offending satirists from live appearances on every television and radio station in the country under pain of loss of licence.

One particularly obscene word had been used. "Something a lot of us sit on," Dudley later explained to the National Press Club. "Not a chair. Short word. Starts with 'b', ends with 'm'."

I was 18 at the time, in my first year at Monash University. Student protest was at its height, and when the terrible two appeared on campus, fresh from their monstering by the forces of wowserdom and cant, they were greeted as heroes. The allocated venue filled to capacity within minutes of the doors opening. Speakers were rapidly set up on the lawns. When these proved insufficient for the crowd, lectures were cancelled and the show was piped campus-wide on closed-circuit television.

In the 15 years since, Pete and Dud had plumbed the scatological depths as Derek and Clive, then gone their separate ways. Dudley became Hollywood's resident sex thimble, starring opposite Bo Derek in *10* and playing someone not entirely unlike himself in *Arthur*. Peter made some middling to bad movies and created one of the funniest, most biting satirical speeches ever written, a monologue parodying the judge's summing up in the trial of Jeremy Thorpe, that "self-confessed player of the pink oboe", who once headed Britain's Liberal Party.

"Whereupon," Peter put it, "I immediately did nothing."

Nothing which—miracle of miracles—included agreeing to return to Australia for a week as the official guest of honour of the Melbourne Comedy Festival.

As he staggered from his London flight, fabulously dishevelled, golf sticks slung over his shoulder, partner Lin Chong at his side, the assembled comediocracy of Melbourne could scarcely refrain from prostrating itself at his feet. "You come as an emperor," declared producer John Pinder, "to accept the homage of your subjects."

With the wryly amused air of an infamous rake being invited to inspect a mining camp bordello, he allowed himself to be duchessed around town, making guest appearances, dispensing trophies and generally enjoying the hospitality of the burgh.

The mischief began almost immediately. As he checked into his hotel, he was informed that its manager, lately of Zurich, had requested an autographed photo for the celebrity guest wall of the cocktail bar. Peter immediately launched into an impromptu dissertation on the contribution of Swiss hotel management to the development of modern comedy. Was not the knock-knock joke invented by a Swiss housemaid, he asked? And that mint-on-the-pillow idea was sheer comic genius.

Drawn by the chortling, the manager bustled across the lobby and joined us, a look of comprehension settling on his face. This must be his celebrity guest, the famous English clown. Peter, oblivious to the identity of the man in the pin-striped trousers, continued his monologue. Herr Metzger, taking his cue from the rest of us, roared with laughter. While he was in charge, nobody could say the Swiss didn't recognise a joke when they heard one.

Then it was off to the Town Hall for lunch with another fan, Lord Mayor Trevor Huggard. They talked architecture and His Honour, an early champion of urban conservation, mentioned plans to restore the Regent Theatre, then derelict. It took little encouragement from Peter for the keys to be found and the two of them spent the afternoon wandering through the picture palace's cobwebdraped rococo smoking lounges, Roman Empire Wurlitzer pit and late medieval projection box. It was just the place, Peter decided, for the world premiere of his forthcoming musical based on the secret diaries of Queen Victoria's gynaecologist.

The high point of Peter's official agenda was the press conference to launch the festival, a task he shared with Barry Humphries,
the festival patron. Humphries appeared in the guise of the salivat-
ing, varicose-nosed Sir Les Patterson. It was the big-ticket draw of
the day. All the networks sent camera crews and a seething mass of
journalists packed the room. When the terrible two walked in, all
the photographers popped their flashes simultaneously, triggering
a thermo-nuclear explosion. Peter, rendered the colour of cheddar
cheese by the glare, and beaded with perspiration from the heat of
the sun guns, sat in benign bemusement while Humphries basted
him with reminiscences of their early careers.

At the crack of dawn the next day, Peter and John Clarke
headed for the nearest golf course at 11am in deference to Cook's
customary routine. "My driving hasn't been very good lately," Cook
warned. "But my short game is among the shortest on Earth."
Positively glowing with ill-health, he wheezed his way through 18
holes, club in one hand, Dunhills in the other.

Although an invitation had been issued by Royal Melbourne,
Peter's stated preference was for somewhere a little less starchy.
Clarke took him to Yarra Bend, a public course favoured by off-
duty taxi drivers and shift-working bakers. As they neared the club-
house, Peter spotted a player who had taken off his shirt. He
demanded to see the pro. If people were allowed to wander about
half-naked, he complained, the course should post a notice to that
effect. "Had I known, I would not have bothered wearing clothes."

One of the festival's main attractions was a somewhat anarchic
mock trial, organised by a bunch of barristers and conducted in the
magistrate's court. Spirited away by a team of admiring lawyers and
fed a persuasive lunch, Peter agreed to appear as a judge one night.
He did so in full regalia with a bottle of gin on the bench in front
of him. Presented with a farrago of trumped-up charges and fabri-
cated evidence, he had no hesitation in handing down his verdict—

half extemporised nonsense, half reprise of his Jeremy Thorpe monologue. "The sentence I am about to hand down is sponsored by
Tanqueray gin," he sombrely pronounced. "You always get a result
with Tanqueray."

As might be imagined, my minderly duties were far from
onerous. They consisted principally of dragging an ever-amenable
Peter away from one cluster of admirers and delivering him to
another. Then came the "abscess incident".

Since early in the festival, I'd been conspiring with Lin, Peter's
partner, to protect his liver from the excesses of Australian hospitality. A few days before their departure, Lin confided that Peter was
suffering from a persistent toothache. Self-medication was keeping
a lid on his discomfort, but she was worried that his condition
would not be improved by the long flight home. Could I recommend
a reliable dentist?

Peter was duly chivvied into a taxi and dispatched to my own
dentist in nearby Carlton. Lin remained in their hotel room and
I returned to the festival office, awaiting the call to pick him up.
Awaiting and awaiting and awaiting. Finally, I gave the dentist a
call. An abscess had been discovered in Peter's root canal, I was
told, and he'd been referred on to a specialist in Collins Street.
Who, it transpired, had forwarded him to a nearby colleague. Poor
Peter, it seemed, was being passed around the fang mechanics of
Melbourne, all of them keen to have a dig at his gums. As of last
report, he'd been drained dry, shot full of drugs and ordered back to
his hotel to rest.

But according to Lin, waiting in their room, he hadn't arrived.
With a mounting sense of panic, I pictured an anaesthetised Peter
Cook, his mandible throbbing, wandering the unfamiliar streets in
a daze.

I sprinted the length of Collins Street, scanning the crowd for
a tall Englishman with dribble dripping from his chin, and made
my way to the Regency. Still no sign. What I needed was a quick

something to settle the nerves. And that's how I found him, perched at the far end of the otherwise empty cocktail bar, a vodka tonic in front of him and a pensive Dunhill between his fingers.

Feigning nonchalance, I parked myself on the stool beside him and inquired as to his dental health. He gave a casual shrug, then reached into his mouth and removed what appeared to be a brand-new cricket ball. On closer examination, this turned out to be a huge wad of blood-soaked cotton wool. He took a sip of his drink, a deep puff of his cigarette and allowed that it might be best if he had a little lie down, if only to assuage Lin.

What was needed, Lin decided, was a day in the country. Exposure to the therapeutic qualities of the bush would do him a world of good. Hanging Rock seemed just the ticket, the perfect spot for an afternoon's escape from the attention of the press, the importunings of entertainment producers and the attentions of over-excited fans. The autumn countryside was lush with ripening grain and the vines were heavy with grapes. Here, at last, was the pay-off for the trip. A decent lunch was had at Macedon and Hanging Rock was ours alone, the towering boulders looking as eerily compelling as they had in Peter Weir's film. You could almost hear the pan pipes. A sign at the foot of the hill advised that any wildlife encountered should be treated with caution. Peter wondered if he should have brought condoms.

He ascended the path slowly, alert for evidence of promiscuous fauna. "If we get to the top and there's a camera crew waiting," he muttered, "I'll fucking well kill you." But the only camera was Lin's. As she snapped the view from the top and Peter lounged like a satyr among the boulders, I did my best to rustle up a koala.

I am not, I daresay, the first of my countrymen to be urinated upon by a marsupial. But I am probably the only one who had Peter Cook there to witness the event. Ten metres above me, with unerring accuracy, a slumbering fur ball opened its bladder. Peter, well out of range, roared with amusement.

And for that, I will remain eternally grateful to that anonymous arboreal incontinent. Stoned out of its tiny mind on eucalyptus leaves, it probably didn't even notice the look of satisfaction on my face. So what if I was doused in koala piss? I had made Peter Cook laugh.

In London a year or so later, I had dinner with Lin and Peter. She was still trying to get him to take better care of his health. But longevity was never a priority for a man who had done everything he ever wanted by the time he was 21 and who tended to the view that a bit of what you fancy does you good. Eventually, in January 1995, his liver threw in the towel.

Thanks to the publicity boost generated by his presence, the inaugural Melbourne International Comedy Festival was a major success. For 10 days, a kind of delirium gripped the town and any absurdity seemed possible. At the festival's closing event, the Fools' Ball, Peter presented the prize for the best costume. One table arrived dressed as the Harold Holt Memorial Swimming Pool, but the winner was a heavily pregnant woman attired as an elephant. Her perfect prize was two dozen bottles of pink champagne.

It just so happens that that elephant was my wife. Our daughter, born two weeks later, accompanied me to every festival gala opening from the time she was 10. But she's grown up now, out in the world. On the eve of this year's event, she sent me an email from Medellin, Colombia. The previous night she had been partying at a club where the waiters were dwarfs dressed as Santa, the bouncers were oiled Nubians in harem pants and dusty substances flowed with carefree abandon. It sounded like a Peter Cook kind of place.

ALEXANDER DOWNER

The satire we had to have: Keating

It's back! *Keating! The Musical* returns to Adelaide, updated and slightly more sophisticated than the original. This is good news for that 20–25 per cent of the population who loved and probably still love Paul Keating. It's also good news for those South Australians who think: (a) Bob Hawke is a terrible spiv who shamefully held on to power for too long when he should have handed over to the flamboyant genius Keating; (b) that John Howard was a hideous, ghastly, cynical megalomaniac unworthy of office; (c) John Hewson was a feral abacus; and (d) Alexander Downer is a sexually ambiguous son of the Adelaide Establishment.

Unsurprisingly, I don't happen to think any of those things about those people, knowing all the dramatis personae as I do.

But the truth is this musical is fun. It's a celebration of Keating's political career combining satire with history wrapped up in music.

If some people's political sensitivities are offended by the portrayal of some of our better known, better loved and often loathed politicians, they shouldn't be. This is satire. It's not an attempt to portray anyone as they really are, with the possible exception of Keating.

And let's face it: It's funny. Since the time of the ancient Greeks, the great and powerful have been lampooned and ridiculed and it's good for them and good for society that they are.

Britain is well served by an often hilarious satirical scandal sheet called *Private Eye*. It's disrespectful, iconoclastic, revealing and funny.

In Australia, we sometimes take ourselves a bit too seriously. People in high office should always take their jobs seriously but not themselves. Australian newspapers and magazines are seldom amusing—although for some reason we have among the best newspaper cartoonists in the world. So *Keating! The Musical* is a rare and refreshing addition to Australian political humour and satire. And it's very well produced and presented.

For a musical which celebrates the Keating years, it does reinforce your prejudices. Some loved the boy from Bankstown emerging in Zegna suits all made in Italy. It was so gloriously ... well ... stylish. They could identify with a prime minister who wore as a badge of honour his disdain for sport. I remember Keating famously saying that in rugby you "kick a try". Hmmm.

Some loved his vanity, which is starkly presented in *Keating! The Musical*. We are reminded of his self-assessment as the Placido Domingo of Australian politics. This vanity is nicely presented in the song "I'm the Ruler of the Land". Some loved these Keating characteristics but most didn't.

Watching *Keating! The Musical* made me wonder why Keating made such a public display of his eccentric self-assessment and his passion for the so-called finer things in life. Most successful people have enormous self-confidence and self-belief. They do think they're pretty clever.

But they're clever enough not to tell everyone. Why would they feel they had to? Why would Keating feel the need to tell a bunch of journalists that Australia had never been blessed with a decent prime minister but that he was the Placido Domingo of Australian politics?

Love of Mahler's music is not common, but then again it's not all that unusual. I like Mahler myself and have it on my iPod. But why is it necessary to boast about your love of Mahler and sneer at those who might prefer Silverchair or the Arctic Monkeys (not on my iPod)? I call my children "music fascists" because if you don't like their music, they laugh at you and turn it up. And they turn mine off. Well, there's a touch of the music fascist about Keating. *Keating! The Musical* reminds us also of Keating's great causes. He became obsessed with the republic and "Asia"; not interested, obsessed. Keating had only been to Asia once as treasurer and that was to Japan. By the time he became prime minister, he decided all these countries he'd never been to were front and centre of our national being. I've heard of the zeal of the convert but this was something else.

It was all about our identity, as though we had no identity at all. People went along with this for a while, feeling that to object would invite abuse, denigration, ridicule and a fusillade of personal insults. That was the thing about Keating: the insults. I had a teacher who used to say that personal abuse was what you resorted to when you had exhausted all your intellectual arguments.

Well, Keating didn't even start with intellectual arguments. It was all slogans and abuse. Surely, I used to wonder, he could find some good, some merit in his political opponents. No, he couldn't.

The thing about *Keating! The Musical* is it reminds us so vividly of one of our most colourful and least popular prime ministers. It's worth making a musical about him because he was such a controversial and unusual character.

Go to see the musical. It's excellent entertainment: It's funny, it's well performed, the tunes are catchy and it will massively reinforce your assessment of Keating. If you thought he was a great and colourful visionary, it's all there. He tells you he was. If you thought he was a tosser, the Sir Edmund Hillary of social climbing, a faintly unbalanced personality, that's there as well.

Whatever you think of Keating, this is the show for you.

GERMAINE GREER

So Ian McKellen drops his trousers to play King Lear. That sums up the RSC's whole approach

The most memorable moment, for many of us the only memorable moment, in Trevor Nunn's latest production of *King Lear* is when Ian McKellen drops his trousers and displays his impressive genitalia to the audience. To get the full beauty of this sublime coup de théâtre, you have to understand that the 1,000-strong audience is composed of a minority of geriatrics who haven't got out of the theatre-going habit, and a majority of teenaged school-trippers bussed in from various grim hostelries in the environs of Stratford. Most of the members of the audience don't have English as their first language. This matters less because the Royal Shakespeare Company long ago gave up simply saying the lines for mouthing, gnashing, yelling, snarling, munching, spitting, gritting, grinding, shrieking, slobbering, snapping and gobbling them. The only actor in this production who dares to speak clearly enough for the greatest metaphysical poem in the English language to make itself momentarily heard is William Gaunt as Gloucester, who, in a mere six lines of recognisable iambic pentameter, reduced this patron to tears.

McKellen displays his usual astonishing repertoire of gesture and movement; he begins with hand tremors signifying eld, proceeds to spastic arms and rubbery hands, totters and teeters, grunts, gapes and squints, until he is as irritating as any fractious, befuddled, sclerotic old bugger you've ever met. McKellen's method has always had more to do with impersonation than interpretation. His Lear is so tottery, closer and closer to capsizing in every scene, that we watch fascinated by the wrong things. Such virtuosic caricature makes sympathy impossible. King Lear is certainly a play about entropy, about ageing, decay and loss, but we cannot approach its inner meaning through a simple replication of aged behaviour. At the very point when McKellen mightily distracts his audience by exposing himself, Lear is realising that kingship is a delusion, whether it be sovereignty over a state or over oneself. If we do not look with him through the windows of awareness that open in the verse, watching King Lear is a waste of precious time. We love Lear because he is not confused enough to be unaware that he is confused. We will not be the more stirred by his death because of the accuracy of McKellen's horrifyingly authentic rendition of a death-rattle.

The production is as perverse as anything Trevor Nunn has ever done. We are back in Ruritania, much as we were in his 1976 production, with operetta uniforms and occasional bursts of operetta music. There is lots of noise, very loud noise—shots, thunderclaps, total war and brain-churning organ chords—anything to stop you hearing the words. The Fool combines rather too much of his wordplay with playing the spoons. The permanent set looks as if it might come in useful for a revival of *The Phantom of the Opera*, except that the upper galleries are never used. Nunn means Lear's progress to be a journeying "away from the pampered luxury of the court", but there's no getting away from this set. The only way to suggest the heath is to dim the stage to almost black and shower it with water.

Most irritating is an interpolated scene in which the spoon-playing Fool is hanged on stage. This is the only time that the vertical space was used, thank God. To choruses of grunts and snarls from the Ruritanian cavalry, the Fool's harness is hooked up, and he is gently hoisted aloft, arms and legs feebly jerking as if to suggest that his neck had been broken. Like the rain on the stage, the fake hanging was better left out, but when it comes to inexplicable dumb shows, Nunn is your man. Shakespeare's play descended into Grand Guignol so we could all be sent out into the comfortless foyer on some sort of a high. (Dudgeon in my case.) I watched the blinding of Gloucester through my fingers, just in case we had eyeballs bouncing round the stage like ping-pong balls, but we were spared.

Nunn justifies Lear's dropping his trousers as his bid to become "unaccommodated man", which he might as well have done by removing his upper garments, you'd think. (When the trick was tried before, in 1997, by Ian Holm at the National, all his kit came off.) Ben Meyjes, as Mad Tom—who, according to the Folio, is supposed to be naked under a blanket, "else we had all been shamed"—wears a breech clout so fixed that it might have been sprayed on with fibreglass. In 1974, when McKellen played Edgar in King Lear for the Wimbledon Theatre, he seized the opportunity for full frontal nudity: "In preparing my disguise as Mad Tom, I flung off all my clothes and stood briefly on stage as the bare fork'd man. This was a simple image to counterpoint the impenetrable obscurity of Edgar's language."

Edgar's language is our language, our most valuable inheritance. There is no point in our massively subsidised cultural institutions if they devalue our greatest asset by blandly assuming that Shakespeare's language is impenetrable. Edgar does talk fake visionary nonsense but it has a point, one that Nunn and his minions ignored. No wonder we sat unmoved in the Courtyard Theatre as Edgar/Tom, in a crude version of quack aversion therapy, tricked his blind father into jumping from a precipice that wasn't there. There's no way an audience can get the point if the actors are persuaded that there isn't one.

ROD QUANTOCK

Group giggles groovy again

The First Melbourne International Comedy Festival wobbled around the unpredictable presence of comedy's Moses, Peter Cook, who was nursed along by an adoring festival patron, Sir Les Patterson. It boasted 69 shows and promised "1,262,148 jokes, japes, punchlines, pranks, guffaws, grins, giggles and a few puns".

In its 20th year, the obvious thing to say about the 2006 MICF is, "My, hasn't it grown." Its size relative to almost anything, including elephants, staggers those who were there at the start.

Festival 2006 is 160.778 per cent bigger than Festival 1986. That's a better 20-year return than the ASX and as a rate, second only to the growth of China over that time.

This year there are 233 shows and more than 3000 individual performances in 4.2 million venues spread over 53 pages of the *Melway*. These figures are up from an all-time high of 211 shows in 2005, which was up from an all-time high in 2004, which was up from an all-time—well, you get the idea.

(Based on the number of comedians needed to perform the burgeoning shows, it is projected that by 2050, comedians will outnumber audiences and the glut in the apartment market will ease as every available space becomes a venue. That this should happen at the same moment the oil runs out and polar bears become extinct, is perhaps but a happy coincidence.)

If the 1986 festival was the first, it wasn't the beginning. That was somewhere in a disjunction of the space-time comedy continuum that occurred around the introduction of television.

Until the early '60s, theatres such as the Tivoli formed a national touring circuit for musicians, jugglers, exotic dancers, magicians, hypnotists, animal acts, escapologists and comedians. The great George Wallace, Maurie Fields, Chico Marx, WC Fields, Victor Borge and Jimmy Edwards all performed on-stage in Melbourne.

I was too young to go to the Tiv before it closed but I watched its last show broadcast on the medium that killed it.

The passing of the Tiv broke a succession of comedy that could be traced to the music halls of industrial Britain. For the next 10 years, live comedy was off the menu.

Some comedians such as Funny Face Gordon, Maurie Fields, Rosie Sturgess, Ernie Bourne and Joffa Boy made it into the black-and-white world of the box. Lots didn't.

For them, working meant working live, and the only places booking live in Melbourne in the '60s were liniment and lager pleasant Sunday mornings and smoke nights with strippers and 8mm porn. The patter was blue and the ladies, God bless 'em, weren't welcome even if they bought a plate.

Public laughter became private laughter until baby boom comedians, fresh from student theatre (God rest its soul), and disconnected by a generation from their antecedents, did comedy differently, without joke books and writers. They would never think of inviting you to take their mothers-in-law, because they didn't have mothers-in-law. They had other things to talk about, Melbourne things. But there was nowhere to say them.

Until 1974, year zero for Melbourne comedy and the Melbourne International Comedy Festival. In 1974, *Countdown* came to the ABC, ABBA won Eurovision, and Nixon resigned on television while the last US citizens were rescued from Saigon. Cyclone Tracy stopped Santa getting to Darwin, John Howard entered Federal Parliament and Whitlam was prime minister. Just toss in the entrails of a chicken and you've got everything you need to start a comedy revolution.

And that's what happened in 1974 when The Flying Trapeze Cafe appeared, Tardis-like, in Brunswick Street, Fitzroy, and out stepped John Pinder, who promptly put up an "acts wanted" sign. The festival that is Melbourne laughing at itself began that day. Brunswick Street probably started that day too.

Suddenly 40, 60, 80 people a night were leaving their lounge rooms and laughing together. Before decade's end there were hundreds gathered for a giggle as venues bloomed: Foibles in Carlton came and went in flames; the Last Laugh took off with the Barnum and Bailey Pinder; performers started The Comedy Cafe and Banana Lounge; the prince of venues, the Prince Patrick, was open; and the Dick Whittington was the other side of the river with the Espy.

In 1983, *Australia, You're Standing in It* pushed Melbourne comedy through the cathode-ray ceiling and onto the ABC while Pinder was busy lobbying the State Government to fund a festival of comedy. In 1986, the propitious year that Haley's Comet returned, the first Melbourne International Comedy Festival was announced by premier John Cain, wearing a Groucho nose'n'spectacles set.

Names of myth and legend and the household variety populate the first program—Max Gillies, Gerry Connolly, Evelyn Krape, Barry Dickens, Los Trios Ringbarkus, Wogs Out of Work, The Cabbage Brothers, Lawyers Guns and Money, Let the Blood Run Free, Funny Stories, Linda Gibson, Combo Berko, Gina Riley, Maryanne Fahey, Wendy Harmer, The Hot Bagels and The Doug Anthony All Stars.

That first year a women-only show, *La Joke at Le Joke*, was a hit and every festival since has had a women-only performance.

"Cartoonists Speak" started something too that year and exhibitions of cartoonists have been part of most festivals.

There was a cake exhibition in 1989 at the Arts Centre, featuring cakes made to look like famous celebrities. Hills hoists decorated in-situ graced the 1990 festival. There was an unfulfilled scheme of then director, Shane Maloney, to run seminars in the City Square for garden gnomes who could be dropped off by their owners on their way to work and retrieved at the end of the seminar day happier and wiser gnomes.

Subsequent years saw John Clarke's attachment to the written word beget *Humourists Read Humour*. This year, the Annual Comedy Debate turns 16.

Every year since, the festival has had its stayers, its newcomers, its up-and-comers and its faders. A lot has been lost or changed in those 20 years. Today, the Fly Trap is a Japanese restaurant, and strangely, so is The Comedy Cafe. The Last Laugh is a bar. The Prince Patrick is an up-market pub and the Espy is a VCAT decision. The Universal Theatre is—well I haven't dared look.

In *The Graduate*, Dustin Hoffman was advised to get into plastics. Today he would be told "comedy", judging by the number of people who enter for *Class Clowns* and *Raw Comedy*.

These contestants do what everyone dreads—get up on stage in front of stingers and make 'em laugh. And most of them do.

Those who can do a "tight five" through the heats and semi-finals and make it to the final can expect a long apprenticeship if they want to stick it out. It might be fun, but there are less live options now and many more live comedians.

Between festivals, the opportunities to run your tight five are few and the competition for stage time fierce. The aim is to go from that tight five that wowed the judges to a tight 10, then 15, then it's the Comedy Festival. Can you do an hour? Can you do it three, four or more years in a row until noticed?

Despite the success of the festival, it has never been harder to survive in comedy. Working means a night here, a night there, sometimes for money, mostly not. The smell of the grease paint and the roar of the crowd are an addictive concoction and people will work for nothing. Because if you do make it, the rewards are enough to make your parents stop nagging you to finish your law degree.

This year, as a judge of some heats of *Raw* and *Class Clowns*, I have already seen two or three who could make a go of it. You should see them too. I know you have your must-see favourites and you spent a lot at the Commonwealth Games and you're worried about your AWA, but if the budget will stretch, go and see someone you've never seen, someone you may never want to see again or someone who will one day look back at you from your flat plasma screen as they take home the gold Logie or Nobel Peace Prize. If you can't see them during the festival, track them down in the 11-month off-season. They'll enjoy it and so will you and between-festival comedy may just boom again.

Business

GIDEON HAIGH

Packed it in: The demise of the *Bulletin*

Few Australians have loitered so long at the brink of death as Kerry Packer, and perhaps none so ambivalently. Tens of millions of dollars were lavished on the campaign to prolong his life. He was saved first by timely defibrillation, then by a transplanted kidney, and finally by a constant cycle of surgery and steroids, trailed everywhere by the best minds in clinical care. But, heedless of the medical consequences, Packer was resolved to make no changes to his life whatsoever. The addiction to junk food remained unaltered by diabetes; the smoking continued unabated, despite six coronary angioplasties. "Light my cigarette, son," he famously told a prominent cardiologist. Upbraided for his lifestyle by a specialist at the Cornell Medical Center, he made his priorities perfectly clear: "All right, son, you've given me the fucking lecture … Now are you going to fucking fix me up or aren't you?"

No title in Packer's print empire was closer to his overtaxed heart than the weekly *Bulletin*. And in its last two decades, no title seemed quite so shaded by its proprietor's personality. Tens of millions of dollars were allocated to the *Bulletin*'s survival. There were constant transfusions of journalistic talent and executive expertise. There were regular relaunches and recalibrations. But the venerable masthead, dedicated to the week's news, geared to rapid response, found it hard to break the habits of a lifetime, and out-lived its legendary master by barely two years.

On the morning the *Bulletin* finally closed, Thursday, 24 January 2008, editor-in-chief John Lehmann went for a haircut. There were bound to be television cameras; he might as well look his best. Lehmann was right. The news crews duly came, but they camped out the front of ACP Magazines, at 54 Park Street, Sydney, un-aware that for four and a half years the *Bulletin* had been round the corner in Stockland House, at 175 Castlereagh Street. It was a happy accident allowing *Bulletin* employees to stroll mainly un-molested to their impromptu wake at Darling Harbour's Pier 26; it also attested the magazine's marginal position in the Australian media.

Newspapers the next day rushed to tell the story of the suits at CVC Capital Partners, who now control ACP Magazines through the 75% stake in PBL Media they secured last year, and who had now trampled the traditions of 128 years. "Welcome to the brave, but soulless, new world," said John Lyons (former *Bulletin* national-affairs editor) in the *Australian*. "It was the last bastion of the long view," said Tony Wright (former *Bulletin* national-affairs editor) in the *Age*. At word that the *Bulletin* was losing about $4 million a year, eyes moistened in memory of the dear departed. "Kerry would win or lose that [$4 million] in a weekend in Las Vegas or London," observes David Haselhurst, for 35 years the stock-tipper extraordi-naire behind the magazine's "Speculator" column. "The money the carpetbaggers [CVC] were losing in the *Bulletin* was an eighth of what they had just paid themselves in executive bonuses," notes Patrick Cook, for 20 years the voice of its satirical "Not the News" page.

Squirming at the scrutiny, the venture capitalists proceeded with a hugger-mugger interment. The magazine's website was switched off within a day. Its name was swiftly removed from the downstairs listings at Stockland House, while mail was soon being returned to senders with blunt stickers advising, "NO LONGER AT THIS ADDRESS ... *BULLETIN* CLOSED." On the day I visited, the door of the magazine's eerily silent office was still blazoned with its last cover, "Why We Love Australia".

Yet there's no doubt that this passion of the *Bulletin*'s was, towards its end, unrequited. Audited circulation had halved since the 1980s, its ageing subscribers were not being replaced and its newsstand visibility had dwindled. When one former senior staffer sought a souvenir of its last edition at Central railway station on 24 January, he searched a big newsagency high and low, to no avail; finally asking for help, he was directed to two copies hidden almost out of sight.

Schadenfreude is always possible when one magazine reports the closure of another with which it is widely supposed to be in competition. That's not the case here: this writer enjoyed a happy decade as a contributor to the *Bulletin* and counts a number of former employees as friends. In studying the decline and fall, nonetheless, you can't help hearing the echo of its erstwhile proprietor's famous deathbed comment: "Am I still there? How fucking long is this going to take?"

~

The last 18 months of the *Bulletin*'s deathbed vigil had been gruelling. There was a sense, in some of its more panting covers, of a publication running hard to stand still. There had been a constant cycle of farewells, 20 staff reading the signs and moving on. Most of the senior staff members were replaced by less seasoned reporters, where they were replaced at all.

Much of Lehmann's time had been devoted to doing more with less, sometimes with nothing at all, as when he invited politicians to contribute to the *Bulletin* during the election campaign. "Who can I get?" was the question by which he became known. Sometimes this had an unconscious comedy. "Who can I get to do a cartoon?" he said, emerging from his office one day, apparently oblivious to his having just let go his last two cartoonists.

In these austerities he was watched over by his publisher, Paul Myers, a short, bossy figure installed by PBL Media CEO Ian Law, who had previously run the RM Williams magazine, *Outback*. Myers might have fitted in a century earlier, when the *Bulletin* had rejoiced in its reputation as the "Bushman's Bible"; staff now referred to their cheeseparing publisher as "Small Pliers". Some economies were noticeable, such as the replacement of Jana Wendt as "Lunch with" columnist by the lighter and less costly Juanita Phillips; some seemed niggardly, like canning *The Chaser*'s droll headline news summary. Others became the stuff of legend. Book reviewers? Who needed them? "Why do we have to pay these people?" griped Lehmann one day. "Don't they like reading?" Myers stormed: "We've got 26 people on staff! Get one of them to do something!"

The *Bulletin*, nonetheless, had soldiered on, and continued to punch above its diminishing weight. Its ace Darwin correspondent, Paul Toohey, broke the story of Therese Rein's business interests; its dogged investigator Jennifer Sexton revealed the shady past of Paul Keating's business associate Bruce McDonald, and the bizarre mores of Rene Rivkin's inner circle. The magazine had unearthed one excellent young reporter, Katherine Fleming from *Medical Observer*, and manufactured another, Joey Catanzaro, promoted from manning the front desk to touring Iraq. By the end of last year there was the kind of euphoria that comes from having apparently cheated the hangman. Cook remembers that where the Christmas lunch of 2006 had been "thinly attended and resentful", that of 2007 had involved "a vast amount of enthusiasm, goodwill and yippee". So, despite all the grim tidings, it came as a shock when group publisher Phil Scott introduced ACP Magazines CEO Scott Lorson in the *Bulletin* office that Thursday morning.

Lorson arrived like a man bearing bad news—dark suit, navy blue shirt, scuffed loafers—and wasted no time sharing it. He herded staff into a tight group in front of him, as though they were soldiers on parade or children at a school assembly, and told them they had published their last issue, efforts to sell the magazine having failed. Phones in the office were ringing before he had finished his address: a press release announcing the closure was already in circulation. How long did it fucking take? In the end, about 20 minutes. In hindsight, probably closer to 20 years.

~

During his three vigorous years as editor-in-chief of the *Bulletin*, Lehmann's predecessor, Garry Linnell, toyed occasionally with the strapline "Setting Australia's Agenda Since 1880". His news editor, Tim Blair, would laugh: "Are you sure you want to remind people of some of the agendas we've set?" After all, earlier straplines had included "Socialism in Our Time"; then "Australia for the Australians"; and, most infamously, "Australia for the White Man and China for the Chow".

For much of its history, the *Bulletin* was chauvinistic to the point of isolationism, denouncing foreign wars and foreign capital with equal ardour; it was also unblinkingly anti-British, especially when the empire was in its view insufficiently racist. "There is nothing to lead us to believe," it editorialised a hundred years ago, "that [John] Bull, bloated with pride over the possession of over 300,000,000 nigger subjects, has a vestige of sympathy with, or comprehension of, the White Australia ideal." It was variously anti-Semitic and anti-communist; it was content to yield Spain to Franco, and Italy to Mussolini; it advised appeasement of Hitler ("Far from being a megalomaniac," said the *Bulletin*, three weeks before the invasion of Poland, "Adolf Hitler is probably the most modest man in Germany") and counselled scorn for Churchill ("Mr Churchill is the Dangerous Dan McGrew of Imperial politics," said the magazine in January 1940, "and he is far more dangerous to us than to the enemy").

At its best and boldest, however, the *Bulletin* was more than a periodical. "It was *Australia*," said the writer–adventurer Randolph Bedford. DH Lawrence's alter ego, Richard Somers, exempted the *Bulletin* from his drear view of Australian culture in *Kangaroo* (1923): "He liked its straightforwardness and the kick in some of its tantrums. It beat no solemn drums. It had no deadly earnestness. It was just stoical and spitefully humorous." There were the writers: not just Henry Lawson and Banjo Paterson, but Steele Rudd, CJ Dennis, Joseph Furphy, John Shaw Neilson, Dorothea Mackellar, Katharine Susannah Prichard, Frank Dalby Davidson, Christopher Brennan, Ethel Turner, Barbara Baynton, Vance and Nettic Palmer. There were the artists and cartoonists: Hop (Livingston Hopkins), Phil May, Norman Lindsay, Fred Leist, Will Dyson and David Low. "Perhaps never in the history of world journalism has a paper stood nearer to the heart of a country than the *Bulletin*," thought Sidney Baker, who studied the publication intently for his classic *The Australian Language* (1946). "Perhaps never again will so much of the true nature of a country be caught up in the pages of a single journal."

Every journal has a lifespan, of course, and founder JF Archibald had no illusions about the *Bulletin*'s, foretelling that his "clever youth" would inevitably "become a dull old man". His prophecy seemed to have been fulfilled 50 years ago, when the *Bulletin*'s circulation was barely 27,000, having more than halved since World War II, burdening the Prior family, its owners since 1927, with heavy losses. Its survival was a fluke. Frank Packer, publisher of the *Daily Telegraph* and impresario of Channel Nine, wanted to neutralise the Priors' *Woman's Mirror*, a rival to his own *Australian Women's Weekly*. Packer was not quite sure what to do with the unprofitable, inert *Bulletin*, which came as part of the purchase, in October 1960. He rang Donald Horne, editor of his new fortnightly, the *Observer*. "I've bought the *Bulletin*," he said. "Which will we kill off? It or the *Observer*?" The *Bulletin* endured on Horne's whim: it was, if you like, the Lucky Publication.

The *Bulletin* scarcely deserved its good fortune. Horne found it "a clumsy souvenir of long ago", printed on inferior stock, sustained by infestive readers: "Of the dozen and a half jokes in each issue ... there was always an 'Abo' joke, and often a reffo joke, although the reffos no longer had Yid noses, but the largest single category was jokes about the daftness of old women and the bodily curves of young women." Horne rewrote its manifesto, committing it to give "an informed picture of the life we lead in this country and its extraordinary diversity", and forbore the frenzied hostility of the response to his changes: at least one reader sent several used pieces of toilet paper.

Horne's two spells as editor, separated by the tenures of Peter Hastings and Peter Coleman, more than doubled the circulation. The editorships of Trevor Sykes and Trevor Kennedy doubled it again, seeing off challengers like Gordon Barton's *Nation Review* and John Fairfax's *National Times*. The by-lines were as bejewelled as Barry Humphries, Xavier Herbert, Hal Porter, Thomas Kenneally, David Williamson, Frank Moorhouse and Gwen Harwood (who took her leave with piqued acrostics whose first letters spelt S-O-L-O-N-G-B-U-L-L-E-T-I-N and F-U-C-K-A-L-L-E-D-I-T-O-R-S). Few Australian journalists of note, meanwhile, did not serve at least a brief tour of duty at the magazine, including some with big plans. Wannabe Labor player Bob Carr never stopped networking: he used his position as state political roundsman to introduce the likes of Paul Keating, Graham Richardson and Barrie Unsworth to his proprietor. Aspiring conservative politician Tony Abbott was known for his iron discipline: after running at lunchtime, he would plant his head on a cleared desk, sleep for exactly ten minutes, and immediately resume work. Speaking at Malcolm Turnbull's thirtieth birthday, Kennedy jested that the prime ministership was a mere bauble: Turnbull would be satisfied only by world domination.

The *Bulletin* duly became part of the Packer inheritance that Kerry valued. If he no longer had the *Telegraph* at his disposal, like his old man, the *Bulletin* lent him perceived influence—almost as good, when it came to it, as the real thing. It was fun, too, a sort of knockabout intelligence unit. The scion got to muck about with a few of his father's old retainers, such as Alan Reid and David McNicholl, and to cultivate a few of his own, like Laurie Oakes, a peerless political seer, and David Haselhurst, whose tips for the "Speculator" column outstripped the All-Ordinaries index in 30 of 34 years, including nine years of triple-digit growth.

In the 1970s, in fact, Packer actually trusted Haselhurst to run two investment companies on his behalf, with discretion to place buy-orders up to $40,000. Some might have found the experience of punting their boss's money daunting. The insouciant Haselhurst spent it with abandon, on one occasion leading a plunge into Launceston Gas that inadvertently netted him scrip worth $60,000, the surplus third of which he laid off among *Bulletin* colleagues. It happened that Packer chose that day to whisk staff to Chinatown in four stretch limos, where he was confused by the lunchtime chatter. "Why is everyone talking about Launceston Gas?" the mogul demanded. "I've been meaning to tell you, Kerry," said Haselhurst hastily. "You're now the biggest shareholder there, and we're in it with you." Packer grinned at his minions: "Ah well, when Haselhurst takes me down the gurgler, at least you'll all be coming too." Haselhurst became such a favoured son that when his marriage broke down, Packer lent him $50,000 free of interest to buy a house in Darlinghurst.

Expensive to adequately resource, the *Bulletin* was never massively profitable. And when in the 1980s newspapers invaded the glossy-advertising market by expanding their weekend editions with colour supplements and news reviews, it again became financially marginal. It was even cramping the style of its sister publications. Fairfax, for example, was building a profitable franchise with its *Business Review Weekly*, but Packer dithered over gearing up the fortnightly *Australian Business* as a challenger, out of consideration for the *Bulletin*. For all his personal caprices, Packer was a proprietor who hastened slowly.

To shake the ACP tree, Packer hired Richard Walsh, the former wunderkind of *Oz*, *POL* and *Nation Review* who for the preceding 14 years had run Angus & Robertson. In Walsh's opinion, the magazine market had been changed irrevocably by the arrival of the American news magazines *Time* and *Newsweek*, reliant upon cover prices of almost give-away cheapness to build the circulation that would in turn impress advertisers. But where such businesses could amortise their costs worldwide, the *Bulletin* had only a slow-growing domestic base. The newspaper glossies *Good Weekend* and the *Australian Magazine*, moreover, also had an edge on the *Bulletin*, being spared the newsstand gauntlet by coming out free each Saturday, with a guaranteed circulation. Walsh spent a lot of time considering the *Bulletin*'s predicament and came up with … well, not much. "I couldn't work out how on Earth we were going to get out of it," says Walsh. "When you looked at it logically, there simply didn't seem any strong reason for the magazine to exist."

Above all was the inhibition of his proprietor's conservatism. Walsh's first idea was to eliminate some of the *Bulletin*'s discretionary costs. He planned to merge the commercial, marketing and distribution structures of the *Bulletin* and *BRW* in a 50-50 joint venture with Fairfax, and sell the magazines as a subscription package. Initially interested, Packer cooled on the idea. "Kerry seemed to understand," says Walsh. "Then he decided he would rather lose money." Walsh next reconceived the *Bulletin* as a journal of "vigorous opinion", a weekly in the style of the *Spectator* or the *New Statesman*. He headhunted David Dale—the pithy "Stay in Touch" columnist of the *Sydney Morning Herald* who had written for *Oz* as a teenager at Randwick High School—and mandated him to perk the magazine up. With Fairfax in disarray after Warwick Fairfax's botched buyout, others were willing to follow, among them Patrick Cook, business columnist Glenda Korporaal and photographer Lorrie Graham.

Dale ran a very readable, very attractive magazine. Cheeky covers, a punchy news section called "Reporter", and comprehensive arts, books and entertainment coverage substantiated a McSpedden Carey advertising campaign boasting of the *Bulletin*'s new "brio". But Dale's style and ACP's ways remained oil and water. To Trevor Kennedy, now ACP's managing director, the *Bulletin*'s makeover was too clever, too cute, a little effete. "There's only one thing you need to save this magazine," he lectured. "Fucking good stories." It was the voice of the veteran newsman, at home with scoops, scorchers, bombshells and ball-tearers. Nor did Dale warm to ACP's testosterone-and-profanity-laden culture, where success seemed to be based on "your capacity to fit the word 'cunt' into the sentence more often than the next person". Enemies outside and inside the *Bulletin* were ready to exploit any misstep when Dale gave them opportunity.

In July 1988, Dale and his colleagues selected "The 100 Most Appalling People in Australia", an undergraduate but ecumenical exercise that lumped Paul Keating in with Joh Bjelke-Petersen, Manning Clark with Geoffrey Blainey, Patrick White with John Farnham, with a few *Bulletin* alumni—among them Phillip Adams and Malcolm Turnbull—for good measure. It also included several of Packer's "pick and stick" circle—Alan Jones, John Singleton, Graham Richardson—and news of their displeasure was firmly communicated to Dale. "Kerry didn't read the *Bulletin*," says Walsh. "But he knew people who did." For Packer, the cover resonated with his own impression of news-media negativism, and he inveighed against journalists to one of his loyal foot soldiers, Bruce Stannard, in the *Bulletin* in November 1989: "Unfortunately, many

Australians want to pull down anyone who achieves. And journalists are no exceptions. They have become a law unto themselves."

Dale's attempt to reprise the cover as "The Great Australian Balance Sheet", with assets as well as liabilities, was never likely to endear him to his boss. Today the *Bulletin* of 20 March 1990 reads like a fairly mild survey of *bien-pensant* opinion, with a few disarming twists: John Howard was an asset ("demonstrates a loyalty to party and principle that makes it possible to believe that politics isn't all bad"), Joan Coxsedge a liability ("bores for Australia where possible"). At the time, it loomed rather larger. Most of the barbs were safe enough, like Susan Renouf ("Enouf! Enouf!"); but Singleton was given another touch up ("Good at playing to the lowest common denominator and making a virtue of the vulgar Australia"), while Jones received a rather low blow ("Created an eternal mystery by surviving a spot of bother with the police in London. His friends at home stood behind him").

Uneasy calm prevailed for a few days, and Dale's next issue was one of his most profitable, Toyota paying a premium to buy every single advertisement in the magazine: the sort of deal for which advertising departments break out champagne. It counted not, and the story of Dale's sacking haunts him rather as Sir Peregrine Worsthorne will forever be associated with the story of his sacking as *Sunday Telegraph* editor over perfectly poached eggs on buttered toast at Claridges. When Walsh resigned, rather than comply with Packer's request to sack Dale, Packer did the job himself. "I'm going to fire you," he told Dale. "Can I speak?" Dale asked. "You can speak," Packer replied. "But it'll do you no good."

Walsh has no doubt that Packer loved the *Bulletin*:

> Kerry was pretty much a philistine, but he had his own pretensions. He would scoff, of course, at anything that smacked of high art. But he had a certain respect for Australian traditions, and he understood that his own dynasty was rooted in one of

the golden periods for Australian culture, the period of *Smith's Weekly* and *Australian Women's Weekly*, Ross Campbell, Lennie Lower, Ken Slessor. In that sense he understood the idea of continuity.

But Dale's dismissal was a warning to all his *Bulletin* successors, indeed, all editors at ACP—that in the innovative entrepreneur of *60 Minutes*, *Cleo* and World Series Cricket now beat the heart of a true reactionary.

~

The 1990s were mainly fallow years for the *Bulletin*. Walsh, who was induced to return by Trevor Kennedy, promoted Lyndall Crisp as editor: the first woman to hold the job. But the young James Packer, who had come into the family business as a general manager reporting to Walsh, then advocated the installation of former *60 Minutes* producer Gerald Stone as editor-in-chief. Stone filled the magazine with the flaccid clichés of television current affairs. Apathy prevailed. "Sure, progress brings about great social upheavals but it doesn't change human nature," Stone droned in the *Bulletin*'s 6000th edition, in December 1995. "A good read is a good read." That the world was thoroughly over-endowed with such "good reads" did not seem to penetrate Park Street. The *Bulletin* had Laurie Oakes at one end, Patrick Cook at the other, and David Haselhurst making money in between. Otherwise the magazine stood for an awful lot of nothing in particular; yet the formula was not to be tampered with for almost a decade.

Again, the catalyst was an outsider, John Alexander, former editor-in-chief of the *Sydney Morning Herald* and the *Australian Financial Review*, a news executive with elbows as sharp as his instincts. Joining ACP as group publisher, he made the *Bulletin* a special project—partly, some felt, because he understood it as a short cut to an affinity with his proprietor. Running into Packer at Park Street was a possibility few relished. Not everyone was so poised as Jack Marx, then a senior writer at the *Picture* and *Ralph*, who once found himself in a lift stuck between floors with the mogul and had the presence of mind to say, "I sure hope this lift starts moving soon. I don't know about you, but I've got work to do." But suddenly Packer was to be glimpsed in the *Bulletin*'s office—a sight not seen for 20 years, and an auspicious one now.

Alexander gained Packer's fiat to assemble a hand-picked team of former Fairfax cronies: Max Walsh as editor-in-chief; Paul Bailey as editor; national-affairs editor John Lyons; business correspondents Alan Deans, Deborah Light and Peter Freeman; Melbourne-based feature writers Garry Linnell and Virginia Trioli. These heavy broadsheet hitters he complemented with a gifted magazine specialist. After spells running the *Independent Monthly*, *Rolling Stone* and *HQ*, Kathy Bail had the perfect CV and sensibility to take on the deputy editorship. On the day of her farewell lunch from *HQ*, at Tetsuya's, her mobile rang constantly with calls from Alexander, brimming with bonhomie.

Suddenly the *Bulletin* was the place to work, with big opportunities and salaries to match. One of Walsh's first recruits was Maxine McKew, who had been his co-host on the ABC's *The Bottom Line*, and who now received $3000 a pop for her weekly "Lunch with" column. A former staff member recalls being taken to lunch by Catharine Lumby, who insisted on picking up the bill because she earned more from her fortnightly column than as an associate professor. Contributors accustomed themselves to $1 a word, and the coincidence of the relaunch with the irrational exuberance of the dotcom boom meant that there was plenty to go around. In truth, the magazine still occupied an insecure market niche, and was still spending money faster than it was making it. Former sub-editor Jim Hope recalls, "When we did the first of our big issues, [chief sub-editor] Col Klimo told me that Packer had given an assurance we would not go below 132 pages for at least six months. Within two months we had started shrinking again." But Alexander's close collaboration with Packer did the trick: in March 1999 he succeeded Colin Morrison as chief executive of ACP.

Alexander is cast these days in media circles as the dark prince of Packerdom. Certainly, it is hard to find much affection for him among refugees of the *Bulletin*. "If he decides you're worth knowing, he's all over you," says one. "If he takes a set against you, he's vindictive and spiteful." Says another: "You look at most key media figures in Australia and they've all created *something*. All Alexander has created is a career for himself." This is harsh. At the *Bulletin*, Alexander secured significant resources from a hard-to-please proprietor, and paid talent sometimes-exorbitant tribute. It is arguable, nonetheless, that he was as interested in what the *Bulletin* could do for him as vice versa. For when the *Bulletin*'s unresolved problems re-emerged later, he was a force neither so present nor so positive.

~

Under editors-in-chief Walsh and then Bailey, the *Bulletin* put on an impressively brave face. But the magazine remained a captive of the news cycle: when in doubt, it was always easiest to home in on the week's biggest issue. Such a configuration has advantages: a weekly news magazine can be choosy about what it throws resources at. Yet Australian news is seldom naturally national. As Rupert Murdoch has learned from his stewardship of the *Australian*, a lot of what Australians want to read is local and regional. This funnels the resources of anything with countrywide ambitions towards Canberra, business and sport: fields already amply covered by the metropolitan dailies.

Selling advertising was tough. How did you placate picky advertisers who wanted to know what might be the cover of the edition they supported? News, alas, is unpredictable. And exactly who were you reaching when you placed an ad in the *Bulletin*? The readership was now so fragmented that nobody was quite sure. "The magazine was always sold on the basis that it was read by the powerful, by the influential," says one senior executive. "When you drilled down, there were a lot more Cs [the second-tier demographic, after the much-sought-after ABs] there." The magazine was also eternally beset by its size. As other magazines worked towards creating "'beautiful" and "inspirational" artefacts with edgier layout and higher-quality stock, the *Bulletin* looked increasingly inky and dowdy. The *Bulletin* probably put together the best subs desk in Australia—all full-time staff and all genuine wordsmiths—and had eye-catching artists and cartoonists. But its pages remained obsessively busy, jazzed up with entry points that sometimes had the effect of confusing readers about where to start. The executive with the most magazine experience, Bail, was attractively making over the arts, books and entertainment coverage when space came under pressure with the shrinkage of advertising following the collapse of the tech boom in April 2001, and the last-minute confiscation and cancellation of pages became routine.

Structurally, the magazine seemed stuck in the past. Certainly, it was stuck on Wednesday. That was thanks to the strange archaism of the *Bulletin*'s selection of stories from the American *Newsweek*, an arrangement which dated to July 1984. When it was decided to renegotiate the deal, the original contract was found to be so ancient that it had been prepared on a typewriter. "Everything about the *Bulletin* seemed very old," says *Newsweek*'s assistant editor, Ron Javers. But there was no shifting the *Bulletin*'s publication day without also shifting *Newsweek*'s, and that was never going to happen.

As for the theoretically limitless vistas of cyberspace, the *Bulletin* took one step forward and two back. In August 2001, it launched an online edition on ninemsn, the Packers' joint venture with Microsoft. But it was just that: the *Bulletin* online, which probably cost the magazine more newsstand buyers than it gained. For reasons nobody at the magazine understood, moreover, the online edition was not searchable by Google News, and it was possible neither to blog nor to post pictures much bigger than a postage stamp. The *Bulletin* had access to one of Australia's mightiest pictorial archives—that of the old *Daily Telegraph*—but almost no means of using it.

Only one factor made the *Bulletin* model viable: Packer. His commitment never weakened, and even won him a certain admiration. It made him *un homme sérieux* in the Australian media, as his combustible father had never been. His indulgence, however, was a mixed blessing, for he seemed happier to brazen out losses than to take the chance of succeeding by another means. And in a sense, this rather suited his journalists. Journalists are vain. We will always want to believe that our writing can change the world; that if we break good stories and find the right words, then the market will flock to us as a matter of course. Week in, week out, the *Bulletin* was actually demonstrating that news, in commercial terms, was scarcely worth the trouble of breaking it. When Laurie Oakes divulged Gareth Evans' long-term affair with Cheryl Kernot in July 2002, for example, the *Bulletin* had no way of monopolising the story: such profit as accrued to anyone did so across all news outlets. Yet here was a proprietor who, albeit for reasons less to do with his munificence than with his own distaste for change, apparently subscribed to journalists' belief in the redemptive qualities of their craft. When Packer anointed Garry Linnell as editor-in-chief in December 2002, he issued him resoundingly simple instructions: "Son, just make 'em talk about it." What journalist would not feel their sap rise, given such a charter? The trouble was that the arrangement would never outlive Packer long. The leading indicator of the *Bulletin*'s fortunes in its last years, then, was not its circulation, but Packer's vital signs.

Linnell and his editor, Bail, loved the *Bulletin*. When a portrait of JF Archibald was located on the executive floor at Park Street,

Linnell commandeered it for his office; when readers reported that Archibald's grave at Waverley Cemetery had fallen into disrepair, Bail dedicated herself to its refurbishment. Pound for pound, they marshalled probably the most accomplished journalistic unit in Australia. News editor Tim Blair led a triple life as an acerbic columnist and Australia's savviest blogger. Business editor Alan Deans was a 30-year veteran of the trade from the *Sydney Morning Herald* and *Australian Business*. Features editor Susan Skelly, who had followed Bail from *HQ*, was a former chief sub at the *Australian Women's Weekly* under the legendary Dawn Swain. Together they brought out the most consistently fresh *Bulletin*s since Dale, with a capacity for breaking news that made them compulsory reading in daily newsrooms. Jennifer Byrne prodded Anita Keating into discussing the dissolution of her marriage in April 2004; Tony Abbott acknowledged a lovechild to Julie-Anne Davies in March 2005; Eric Ellis and Preston Smith caught up with fugitive financier Abe Goldberg in November 2005; Paul Toohey owned the Schapelle Corby and Bali Nine stories; the survival of the Beaconsfield miners, Brant Webb and Todd Russell, was recounted in exhaustive detail by Tony Wright. Bail, meanwhile, instigated the *Bulletin*'s "Summer Reading" issues, which brought together long pieces by well-known writers in an attractive perfect-bound package that lingered on newsstands for a month—a formula that was an instant hit. The office enjoyed an enviable esprit de corps. When staff members weren't busy making the *Bulletin*, they were busy talking about it. In the absence of a marketing budget, public-relations man Brian Johnson of Fingerprint Communications arranged scores of radio interviews every week, in which Linnell's reporters trumpeted their work.

In the *Bulletin*'s 125th year, Linnell had the nerve to offer a $1.25-million reward to anyone who found a Tasmanian tiger. But when Packer died at the end of that year, it was the *Bulletin* itself that went from being merely an endangered species to one under threat of extinction. The staff's initial response to the passing of their patron was unforgettable. Without complaint, they returned in droves from summer holidays to assemble a comprehensive and colourful tribute issue, wrangled in three days mainly by chief sub-editor Andrew Forbes. They received a suitably grateful email from the ACP group publisher.

> From: Scott, Phil
> Sent: Thursday, 29 December 2005 7:11 PM
> To: ACP *Bulletin* Mag
> Subject: Thanks
>
> Right now everyone is knackered. Give it a day or two and you will realise you have been part of publishing history this week. Sure, we'd all prefer to have been down at the beach but if we'd stayed there we'd have pondered on what the *Bulletin* should have done to commemorate KP's passing. You should all take great professional and personal pride in the job you've turned around in the last 72 hours. I know the family has been touched by what you have done. The fact everyone wanted to be here to turn this around, without a grumble, has been deeply appreciated. It's a bloody good read and a fitting tribute.

The edition sold out faster than it could be reprinted, scaling six-figure circulation heights not touched in 15 years. It was one of the *Bulletin*'s finest hours, and its last certifiably great one. A little more than two years later, Scott would be introducing Lorson as the bearer of bad tidings.

~

Linnell had run a vibrant, headline-hunting *Bulletin* through three years bulging with big news—the Boxing Day tsunami, the War on Terror, a host of juicy government scandals—without making it essential reading; in fact, tightening circulation audits were eating away the means by which the magazine had previously plumped its numbers. It produced often-excellent journalism, but it was journalism of a sort not uncommon in newspapers. For it is a paradox of the profession that where 2000 words can sometimes be too many, 6000 on the same subject may not feel like quite enough. A thorough professional feature quoting all the relevant individuals on a current news story at the lesser length can never be much more than introductory; by contrast, the nutritious long-form journalism of the *New Yorker* or *Atlantic Monthly* is often inordinately satisfying. The *Bulletin* never confronted the implications of this paradox. "There was a real lack of imagination at the top of the company," says one former executive. "Nobody had the commitment necessary to honestly analyse the *Bulletin*'s problems. Most of the people were out of newspapers who got stressed about news and had no interest in how it was presented. There was this endless bullshit about getting the exclusive, getting the Walkley, then you're a legend." The magazine's dilemmas, notes Tim Blair, were somehow as intractable as they were obvious: "The *Australian Magazine* and *Good Weekend* were coming out on Saturdays. We were coming out five days later, smaller, on poorer stock, with fewer resources. You were always having these conversations about the future direction of the *Bulletin* … but you could never find a way out."

Only once in its last years did the *Bulletin* kick the jams way out—and then, in decidedly peculiar circumstances. In January 2006, with channels Seven and Nine at each other tooth and claw in the C7 action before the Federal Court, *Today Tonight* ran crude recapitulations of the One.Tel fiasco on consecutive nights, singling out James Packer. In his famous affidavit that added "bone" to the media vernacular, Nine's former news and current-affairs chief Mark Llewellyn told of a foam-flecked tirade from John Alexander demanding that collateral damage be inflicted on Seven's Kerry Stokes. According to Llewellyn, Alexander told him: "Nine has failed to go on the front foot previously with Seven and I am sick of that! ... Stokes is a terrible man, and a terrible businessman. Everyone who has come into contact with him knows he is an appalling human being." With his reluctance to comply, Llewellyn apparently marked his card at Nine.

Linnell was interested in a piece on Stokes on his own account, and business reporter Nick Tabakoff did not need to be press-ganged. "Nick heard that they were scouting around for someone to do a big story on Stokes," says a former staff member. "So he went to see Garry and put his hand up, but on condition it did not become a vendetta." It soon became a source of tension. Challenged by his business editor, Deans, about the provenance of the story, Linnell argued with some force that Stokes was a figure of national significance about whom relatively little was known. In the event, the industrious Tabakoff worked for three months on a story that swelled to 15,000 words: from all accounts, a sprawling but fair-minded profile full of hitherto-unpublished information. The piece was then canned, ostensibly for legal reasons to do with the C7 action, although also after Alexander had complained it was "too soft". Bizarrely, a chunk was printed, mangled and manhandled out of context, in an article under the by-line of Tabakoff's successor, Rebecca Urban, formerly of the *Age*, in August 2007—a stage by which events at the *Bulletin* were being dwarfed by events around it.

For with the death of the patriarch, the Packer empire came into play. The fourth Packer, after RC, Frank and Kerry, is the first without regard for print. His chosen route to the sunny uplands of gaming was the staged sale of majority control in PBL Media, incorporating ACP Magazines, Channel Nine and ninemsn, to the Asian arm of CVC Capital Partners, a 25-year-old Luxembourg-headquartered venture-capital firm. Chaos was breaking out. As part of the grab for talent being dispersed, Linnell was wooed as Nine's new news and current-affairs chief, only to arrive on the same day that 95 redundancies were announced. Without a boss, meanwhile, the *Bulletin* looked agonisingly without a future. From time to time over the next six months, a senior publishing executive would breeze into Stockland House and announce that there was no danger of the *Bulletin* closing, which had the same perversely opposite effect as a football club's president stressing his confidence in a coach.

Bail, not only hugely capable but hugely popular, was Linnell's obvious successor. But her relations with Alexander, now chairman of PBL Media, had chilled, for reasons on which nobody was clear: he would not even return her calls. She decided to pitch herself to PBL Media's CEO, Ian Law, formerly CEO of West Australian Newspapers. At a detailed presentation, she explained that the *Bulletin* needed an injection of style: it should free itself from the news cycle and aim to be an up-market monthly, using the "Summer Reading" issue as a model. With a smaller core staff and more contributors, it would be cheaper to run. With the kind of eye-catching design and premium-quality stock that would entice the luxury-goods advertisers that other magazines were tapping so successfully, it should have a better advertising profile. It was as coherent a plan for the *Bulletin*'s resuscitation as had been put—and it fell on deaf ears. When the appointment committee of Alexander, Law, Scott and PBL Media director Chris Anderson made their choice, in July 2006, it turned out to be neither Bail, nor Matt Price, nor Bruce Guthrie, nor any of the other rumoured candidates.

When Scott came into Stockland House to announce that the new editor-in-chief was John Lehmann, there was dead silence. "Nobody could look at Kathy," says one former executive. "Of course, she never lost her sangfroid. But people were shattered." Others detected a latent misogyny at work. "It was horrible, just horrible," says another former staff member. "And so disappointing, because she so deserved to do it. And for women it was a particular blow, because it suggested that a boy was needed to do the job." When Scott left, Blair jumped up and started googling Lehmann's name. Who was this guy? He was little the wiser after the exercise.

Blair was later irked when they met for a drink by Lehmann's airy assertions regarding global warming, not so much because of his views as because someone who purported to read the *Bulletin* closely should have known that Blair was an unapologetic sceptic about anthropogenic climate change.

As an act of courtesy to Lehmann, so that he had time to settle in, Blair, Deans and Skelly mapped out an issue on the anniversary of the Battle of Long Tan. They also shared their disappointment with Scott, and asked if he could do something to make it worth Bail's while to stay—a request at which Scott bridled. "It's my decision," he insisted of Lehmann. "And I'll stand or fall on it." But that wasn't the story that began spreading. Lehmann, it transpired, had come to Alexander's attention while a media writer for the *Australian*. There he had become involved in PBL's interminable politicking, being leaked an exclusive story about Nine CEO Sam Chisholm's attempt to oust John Lyons as executive producer of *Sunday*, an attempt thwarted by Alexander. Shortly before Lehmann departed the *Australian*, he had come into possession of the fabled Llewellyn affidavit. But where *Crikey* published the document— deeply embarrassing to Alexander—Lehmann refrained. He left the paper with the curse of his editor-in-chief, Chris Mitchell, ringing in his ears: "I wouldn't want to be the last editor of the *Bulletin* ..."

Fairly or unfairly, Lehmann was burdened with a reputation as a cat's paw of Alexander and Anderson. Blair became one of the first departures in a steady exodus that soon after included Bail. Into her role as editor slotted the chief sub, Forbes, although into her office moved the publisher, Myers. This was to be the new budget-*Bulletin*, living within slender means. In fact, the new regime made a positive start, responding with alacrity and special issues to the deaths of Steve Irwin and Peter Brock. Lehmann proved to be an irrepressible enthusiast with a well-developed news sense, honed by covering politics in Queensland and crime in New York. He still rallied a good staff. "There were no slow ants or time-servers at the

Bulletin," notes David Haselhurst. "They ran a very lean ship." He also showed some cojones. When the *Australian* ran a powder-puff profile of the Rudds by Mitchell's wife, Christine Jackman, Lehmann had the temerity to reveal that Rudd was godfather to their first son—quite an act of cheek, given Mitchell's legendary capacity for enmity. The *Bulletin* belatedly got its online house in order under Rod Dalton, a former night editor from the *Sydney Morning Herald*: its "Bullring", a site dedicated to the election campaign, was informed and irreverent.

When the news did not provide an obvious direction, however, Lehmann struggled, displaying little aptitude for the *Bulletin*'s non-news component. "We need more celebrities," he would complain. "That was part of my pitch." So it was that the magazine of Lawson and Paterson published an interminable extract from Geoffrey Cousins's business bodice-ripper *The Butcherbird*; *then* it ran an interview with the author; *then* it ran a (deftly non-committal) review. So it was that the magazine of May and Low was reduced to Patrick Cook's weekly cartoon for Oakes's column, but still published a flatulent column by Alexander's friend Leo Schofield. Anything more heterodox was a challenge. On one occasion, Skelly planned to take an extract and photographs from Kaavous Clayton's *Abandoned Chairs*, a whimsical collection of images of discarded chairs in incongruous settings. Lehmann hated it. "We're just not on the same page here!" he barked. "I don't care about chairs!"

Perhaps it was hard to care about chairs when there was a publisher so apt to stress how many feet there were under desks. Myers acted like a census-taker, obsessed with staff numbers. A hundred years earlier, the *Bulletin* had 112 employees; with a workforce a quarter the size, Myers now considered it way too large. He even offered himself as a travel writer. Unfortunately, his prose was execrable. There was universal glee when he left, early in the new year. It was short-lived.

~

Phil Scott took four scenarios to the PBL Media board: sale or closure; business as usual; a radical slimming; a monthly. There was no taste for further cuts, nor was there a zeal for experimentation that might cost money. The bids solicited were circumspect. News Ltd repeated an earlier flirtation with inserting the *Bulletin* in the midweek *Australian*, but pulled back; Lachlan Murdoch probably came closest to putting his hand in his pocket, and might have proceeded had Illyria Holdings not joined the syndicate to take over Consolidated Media Holdings. Yet he would have been caught in the same cleft stick as the Packers. "The problem was that the *Bulletin* no longer had any editorial raison d'être," says one bidder. "If you reformatted the best content in the *Weekend Australian*, *Age* and *Sydney Morning Herald* in any given week, you'd end up with something that looked like the *Bulletin*. As for this revisionist bullshit about Kerry keeping it alive … "

"They stuffed the place up," complained Kerry Packer of the work of his minions at Channel Nine, towards the end of his life. Mistaking money for faith, investment for imagination, he didn't do a bad job of stuffing up the *Bulletin*, the billionaire with such an uncanny sense of public taste in television steadily and obdurately losing his touch with print. Journalists with a sentimental attachment to a proprietor prepared to lose money have let him off lightly, partly because of their collusion in his faltering vision. The *Bulletin* served in concentrated form a news journalism that is now mass-produced—slick but very similar—with which the public is surfeited. Its failure reminds us that what journalists esteem and what readers value are very different things. In the end it took a fucking long time—but it was always going to fucking happen.

FRANK DEVINE

It's a loathe-hate relationship, but at least I own a slice

In my projected memoirs, *Settling Scores: Not a Cricket Book*, I will certainly touch on my life as a Telstra shareholder. Taking into account what I could have earned from investing the money for compounding bank interest over 10 years, I can say I've lost my shoelace on Telstra shares. My holdings are not, nor have they ever been, large enough to threaten my shirt.

True enough I could have made a couple of dollars-a-share profit if I had sold them quickly after accepting the first offer to Telstra customers of shares at $3.30. But, like the other 1.6 million individual owners of Telstra shares and the five million or so dabbling in them through superannuation funds and investment trusts, I was consumed by greed.

This drove me to snap up the second offer of a parcel—well, a thin wad—of Telstra shares at $7.45. Shouting at my computer screen has failed to lift them much above $4.50. There have been dividends, of course, but you don't buy shares in tranches of 600 for dividends, especially not shares in an outfit you hate.

To digress to this matter of hatred, hardly anybody I know is without an ugly memory of Telstra when it was a government-owned monopoly.

Mine involves getting a telephone connection to a new house. Having recently returned to Sydney after several years abroad, I was surprised to learn this would take at least three weeks. That meant nearly a month in which the supplier earned nothing from a new customer, which seemed corporately profligate. When the Telecom technician eventually came, he departed without installing one of the requested plug-in jacks. He returned a week or two later to finish the job and my first awareness of his arrival came from hearing shouting downstairs.

Telecom's emissary was abusing my wife for dobbing him in to his employer for his uncompleted work. His manner was so demented that I stayed home from work for the morning to act as bodyguard and to engage Telecom's man in intermittent philosophical discourse.

When he was finally gone, we discovered—truly and actually—that he had bored a hole in the leg of a chair and run a lead through it.

While appreciating this action, up to a point, as a witty riposte, it did not enhance my confidence in Telecom. I bought Telstra shares partly in the expectation of a profit-driven operation sending forth fewer nutters and furniture molesters.

Telecom's unsavoury reputation has played a part in inhibiting the progress of the company of which I am part-owner. Optus and its associates consider it worthwhile to operate a hate-Telstra website.

In part because its predecessor was so unloved, Telstra has attracted little public support against government attempts to control it, despite having transferred, for a consideration, ownership to me and other investors: in particular, trying to force us to grant competitors access to our fibre-optic network on terms not advantageous to us.

There is a distinct parallel between the behaviour of the government in relation to Telstra and the Bancroft family, former owners of *The Wall Street Journal*, who were eager to grab hold of Rupert Murdoch's US$5 billion but bizarrely insistent on continuing to run the paper.

The reasons for my avariciously anticipating $30 to $50 Telstra shares, and for the institutions considering them such a safe bet, were: (1) as an established entity in an exponentially burgeoning telecommunications market, Telstra was off to a flying start; (2) the fibre connections to the homes and offices of existing and potential customers.

I heard from an unexpected source the other day, a distinguished free-market philosopher, that a case could be made for the fibre network's being public property because it was built with public money. But an incontrovertible argument is surely that ownership of the network came to me and other investors with our Telstra shares, and was a major inducement to us to buy.

My board of directors took the correct tack in rejecting the Rudd government's offer of $4.7 billion towards our providing fast broadband. Reassuringly recognising their responsibility to shareholders, my board said that, if it seemed good business, we would deliver fast broadband ourselves. We wanted no dealings with government consortiums or partnerships, or regulatory threats.

Of course, fast broadband can now be delivered without wires and the government's $4.7 billion might be useful to an entrepreneur taking the wireless path. With our established fibre-optic network, we would, of course, be the first to kick off. That's the market in action.

If it is considered a national need for Telstra to be government-owned again, the government should expect to buy it back from me. If I'm convinced it's in the public interest, I'll take $25 a share.

CHARLES FIRTH

Lies, damned lies

My mum has been lying to me. It's either her or Telstra, and I always take Telstra at its word, so it must be Mum.

This month marks the first anniversary of Justice Peter Gray's ruling that Optus offers better value than Telstra. Telstra had tried to stop Optus running an ad stating that its $49 Cap Plan for mobile phones was superior in value to Telstra's $40 Phone Plan. In denying that request, Australia's third-most senior Federal Court judge said, in words worthy of any advertorial, "It is undeniable that a consumer would get better value under the Optus $49 Cap Plan. Telstra cannot show to the contrary."

I read all of Justice Gray's judgements; he's the Helen Wellings of the federal bench. I assume most Australians read his stuff, given that late last year the number of mobile phones we use topped 20 million, which means that even toddlers are now wandering around with them. Which is why I was surprised to find out that my mother was still on Telstra's $40 plan—the very one Gray had so scathingly criticised.

Mum had asked me to come with her to the Telstra shop to help her get a new phone. Telstra had sent her a "lovely note" urging her to renew her contract on the current plan, for which she would receive $150 in "bonus credits". It didn't mention what bonus credits were, or how they could be redeemed. But $150 credit did sound like a great deal.

She showed me a copy of her latest monthly bill. It itemised 38 calls lasting between 30 seconds and ten minutes. Most of them lasted no more than one minute. For this, she had been charged a total of $87.33, or about $2.30 per call. What was Mum thinking? Had she not seen *Australian Personal Computer*, which featured a long report on the implications of Justice Gray's ruling? Had she not heeded *Choice*'s concise 16-point summary of the pros and cons of pre-paid and post-paid mobile-phone plans?

She admitted that she had been surprised by the size of her bill, especially as Telstra seemed to be charging her twice. After charges for each call, an extra $40 was lumped on top for a service with the line item "Phone Plan $40". The "nice man" at the local Telstra shop had assured Mum that it was a standard charge. On the back of the bill, Telstra told her that she had saved a full $7.81 by being on this plan. At least she wasn't paying $95.14 for 38 calls. *Then* she'd be a sucker.

I asked her who had suggested that she choose this plan two years ago. That nice man at the Telstra shop, she said. It was then that I had an inkling that my mother could lie to my face. For while it is Telstra's right to create a plan that the Federal Court considers to be poor value, it would be deceptive and misleading, bordering on illegal, if the company then pointed unsuspecting customers to that plan and told them it was the best one for their circumstances. Yet this was what Mum alleged.

The idea was absurd. The corporation that sponsors the Paralympics would not deceive a confused retiree by placing her on the worst-value plan in Australia. What would be its motivation? Money? I find it hard to believe that a company with Sol Trujillo in charge would put profit ahead of decency. Sure, according to the latest OECD figures Australia has the third-most expensive mobile-phone service in the world. But Telstra only has a 45% share of the market; it's not as if it exercises huge and anti-competitive power. I've seen the ads: Telstra's just in it for rustic farmers and bronzed surf lifesavers.

I was angry. In the Federal Court case, Optus had alleged that Telstra was pushing its less-informed customers to sign up to deals such as the $40 Phone Plan. I had dismissed these arguments as the rantings of a crazed foreign company—as Telstra points out on its "grass-roots campaign" website www.nowwearetalking.com.au, Optus is foreign-owned. And not just foreign-owned, but Asian-owned. By the Singaporean government. Which is Asian. And foreign.

It was time to expose my mother as a liar, once and for all. Together we walked into a Telstra shop and asked the nice man behind the counter which plan he thought Mum should be on. He looked at her, and then at me. He looked at her bill, and then at me. Without skipping a beat, he said that the Telstra $49 Cap Plan seemed most appropriate. Mum would pay no more than $49 per month. So much for her claim that she had been tricked. I began to suspect that she was foreign. Possibly Asian.

Later that day, as I angrily recounted this tale of motherly deception, my wife suggested that perhaps I was being harsh, that perhaps Mum's confused-yet-affluent demeanour made her seem easy prey during the original transaction, while my confident-yet-devilishly-good-looking demeanour had the opposite effect on the second occasion. And so I decided to give my mother the benefit of the doubt, and to see whether, under different conditions, Telstra would offer me the plan considered worse in value by the Federal Court of Australia.

I needed a double-blind experiment, one in which I couldn't see the Telstra employee and the employee couldn't see me. Also, the results of the experiment would ideally be recorded automatically, to save me the bother of transcribing the interaction later. Luckily, Telstra has devised the perfect tool for this: "Live Chat" online. I clicked on a button on the Telstra website and a window came up, and I was connected to Courtney.

"Hi, how may I help you with your enquiry today?" she typed.

"I don't really know much about phone plans but I want a mobile," I typed back. "Which plan should I get?"

After I outlined what I wanted—to make about 30 calls a month "to my children"—Courtney replied almost immediately with a long description of the $49 Cap Plan, including a series of legal disclaimers. She had apparently typed 146 words in fewer than ten seconds.

"Hang on," I wrote. "Are you human? Or is this a computer talking to me?"

For about 30 seconds there was no reply.

"Yes I am. My name is Courtney and I live in Townsville in QLD," she wrote. My belief in Telstra was renewed. Courtney had *not* suggested the plan that my mother had said she was offered, and was clearly just a very fast typist—on occasion.

"OK, you pass the Turing test. Thanks for your help. I will get a $49 Cap Plan this afternoon."

"If you would like I can organise the plan for you?" Courtney replied.

"That's all right. I would like to do it with the nice man in the Telstra shop."

And with that we parted ways.

I remained curious, and wanted to find out about all the phone plans Telstra has available. In pamphlets I counted 18 different plans, but I had read online that there were others buried in the terms and conditions of some Telstra contracts. Unfortunately, the nice man at the Telstra shop didn't know, so I rang up the company's PR person, Peter Taylor.

The first time I'd called him, it was about Mum's $40 Phone Plan. He'd been brimming with confidence. "You're not going to believe the hype that Optus has put out on this," he had said, before reiterating all the standard arguments about how comparing the $40 Telstra plan with a really bad value Optus plan would be a lot fairer. I'm not sure why Telstra feels this approach makes it look better, but Peter's manner was so reassuring that I nevertheless left the conversation feeling as though Telstra was a little Australian company being bullied by an evil foreign conglomerate, which, Peter reminded me, was Asian, as it was owned by the Singaporean government, which is Asian. And therefore foreign.

When I told Peter that this time I was ringing to find out the number of Telstra mobile-phone plans, his confidence evaporated: "You expect me to know that off the top of my head?" He had a lot of sub-answers: "We have hundreds of plans to suit everyone." But what about the plans hidden in some Telstra contracts? Like the $15 Talk Plan, which is not listed on Telstra's website but has a low call rate, standard text rates and only costs $15 in line rental? "I'll, er, have to get back to you on that one," he said eventually.

Being deceived is a terrible thing. It irks me that my mother would brazenly lie to me. It makes me re-evaluate all the things she has told me in the past. Perhaps it's not true that eating month-old chicken from the fridge will give me a stomach ache. Perhaps motorbikes are safe. Perhaps enlisting in the army *would* be the best thing to do.

The experience has upended my moral universe. But at least I still have one absolute: I know I can rely on Telstra.

Sport

MATTHEW HARDY

Pump more beer, iron out muscle

Grown men who wear fluorescent headbands without irony should make a New Year's resolution to stop.

By grown I mean 19-year-olds, and by men I mean the personal trainers at my gym.

Well, it's as much "my" gym as Jennifer Lopez is "my" wife, but it's still the location of my annual New Year's resolution, which is always to drink less beer and pump more iron. But increasingly I find myself drinking more beer and pumping less iron.

I'm convinced gyms must make the majority of their money from people who've been coerced into a two-year plan during the first week of January, and then, after missing their first session around the middle of March, never return again.

Not returning is one thing, but cancelling your membership is another psychological hurdle altogether.

Aside from the almost $500 fine that most gyms charge you for baling out, actually cancelling a gym membership prevents you from pretending to yourself at least three times a week that tonight or tomorrow is when you're definitely going to renew your regular visits.

So I continue to allow the monthly direct debit to do its incremental damage to my bank account in order to eat that second doughnut after lunch, because I fully believe it will be removed from my expanding waistline as soon as I resume that personally tailored weight program the trainer with the headband went through with me in great detail five months ago.

It's a program the trainer surely knew would not last beyond my local pub's next happy hour, but continued to "create" for me on assessment day anyway, knowing as he must that when we lazy binge-drinkers lie to ourselves, it's best to have a witness.

Therefore the gym gets my cash in return for my absence.

It's a deal I suspect we are both secretly pleased with.

The problem with the gym is that unlike a television documentary on flowers or weather, most of us aren't blessed with the benefit of a life shot in time-lapse photography.

So if we can't see our muscles getting bigger or see our stomachs getting flatter, where's the immediate motive to drink less beer or pump more iron?

There are other things I can't do weights to improve the size of, a fact made obvious by the he-men who insist on strolling around the change rooms stark naked, as if we're all on the same footy team and into the third pre-season of a premiership plan.

Their resolution should be to do a Pat Rafter and wear some comfy undies.

Or any undies!

Or at the very least take the fluorescent headband off, because now you look really stupid.

Big muscle(s) or not.

Any physical progress I ever do feel I might be achieving in the gym is shot down in flames the second I approach the next weight machine and am forced to reach down and place the kilogram pin a whole lot higher in its slot than it was for the previous user.

How can it be possible that I lift less weight on every machine than every person who's used it before me?

And is it possible to do warm-down stretches on top of a fit-ball without feeling certain that footage of your ludicrous attempts will win someone $500 on *Australia's Funniest Home Videos*?

If not, maybe I should concede defeat, film myself and use the money to pay the gym's cancellation fee.

Then I could resolve to take my videos back on time this year instead, before buying six beers and a fluorescent headband to see what the fuss is about.

TONY WILSON

Having a ball: How we finally fell in love with the world game

"He nutmegged him! Archie nutmegged the Argentinian!"

The MCG crowd makes the sound a crowd makes when seventy-odd-thousand people laugh at the audacity of it all. Our Archie, Melbourne's own Archie Thompson, has played the ball through the legs of an Argentine defender and run onto it. Nutmegged him. Those who don't know the word will be learning it; if not in the moment then in the papers tomorrow, when football—the football most of the world knows as football—might once again nudge the front page.

John Vallese from Sunshine is sitting next to me, and smiles in disbelief. Like many of the lifelong fans, he refers to Socceroos games from decades past like tours of duty. We're both in our thirties, but whereas I'm an Iran '97, John is a Scotland '85. But like so many fans, new and old, we were both there for Uruguay 2005.

"That one game in Sydney changed everything," John says of the night the clouds parted, and a benevolent god sent a prophet with the unlikely name of Guus to lead a green and gold army out of the desert. "Hiddink changed it all. Now they actually pass and play properly and try to break down defences. To come here for a practice match and see this many people? I never would have believed it." Tonight, the clouds have organised themselves with the discipline of a Hiddink defence, and a light drizzle is falling, but the crowd is in an ebullient mood. Two girls in the next bay are wearing tiny shorts, gold bikini tops and mobile phone numbers drawn onto their backs. They demonstrate either an opportunistic flair for low-cost advertising or a refusal to concede that Germany 2006, with its white hot football and European sun, can't be sustained for a friendly in Melbourne on a chilly Tuesday night.

It isn't just any old friendly, and that has something to do with the presence of two Argentine superstars: Carlos Tevez and a teenage sensation called Lionel Messi. Messi, the kid who carries the millstone of being the "next Maradona". Messi, whose tiny legs whirr like the wings on a hummingbird, and whose dominance for Barcelona and Argentina has earned him a transfer price of $250 million.

"In a few years you'll be saying you saw Lionel Messi live," John enthuses. Minutes later, Messi surges to the top of the penalty area, the ball stuck to his foot, pauses as the gold socks of Socceroo defenders loom like prison bars, feigns right, no escape, darts left, as elusive as a moth, and cannons his shot into the left upright. Had the ball gone in, it would have been a contender for best goal scored on Australian soil.

"Is the game growing here?" I ask John.

He answers by pointing at a row of kids in front, numbering them off like Von Trapps. "He's soccer, she's soccer. These two: soccer, soccer. These two: Gabriel used to be AFL but is now soccer. My nephew Dominic still says he's AFL but that's just until he thinks of a way of telling his dad …"

"Ohhhhaagghhhhh!"

John is mid sentence, embroiled in family sporting politics when Bresciano's free kick dips onto the crossbar, hits Abbondanzieri in the back of the head, ricochets back to the crossbar, down to the keeper's leg and then trickles wide of the upright. It's an impossible sequence, one that Graham Arnold says he's never seen in 30 years of football. John doesn't see it either, because I have him otherwise occupied yabbering into my microphone. I apologise profusely.

"Oh well, that's soccer," he says. "There's always the replay." We watch it and groan. It could so easily have gone in. A case could even be mounted to say the Socceroos were unlucky to lose. Except we weren't. The Socceroos played attractively and showed all the tenacity that was lacking in the group games at the Asia Cup. But there was an inevitability about the Argentinian goal when it came—a dangerous dipping free kick from Messi, finished with a clinical glancing header by Martin Demichelis. The Argentines didn't seem surprised to be celebrating. Approaching full time, Messi is subbed and the atmosphere is subdued until the scoreboard flashes up the attendance. Immediately the crowd roars, cheering itself as soccer crowds have tended to do in this period of resurgence. 70,171 on a cold Tuesday night. Not bad for a practice match.

~

If the World Cup last year explains the explosion of interest in the Socceroos, it only partly accounts for the fact that Melbourne Victory fans are cheering attendance figures too. The A-League is now in its third season, and crowd averages across the country are a respectable 15,000. Here in Melbourne, however, the numbers are double that, and for a regular season fixture against Sydney last season, more than 50,000 filled the Dome. Throw in league topping and premiership triumphs last season, and it's success bordering on phenomenon.

I'm in the changing rooms, feeling strangely star struck given I only started hearing these names two and a half years ago. Allsopp, Vargas, Pantelidis, Brebner, Caceres. Then of course there are the Socceroo stars: Kevin Muscat, enforcer-turned-sporting ambassador for a city and Archie Thompson, our five goal Grand Final hero, back from dancing the nutmegger suite three days earlier.

"Theo, Theeeee-o" I sing to myself, recalling the terrace chant as I try to comprehend Michael Theoklitos's thighs. He's kicking the ball at young gun Mitchell Langerak who at 19 is judged by many as a Socceroo goalie in the making. But he doesn't have Theo's thighs, will never have Theo's thighs. They are the thighs that propped up the Colossus of Rhodes, the sequoias that keep the Victory defence steady at the back. If the team plane ever goes down in the Andes, heaven forbid—its number one has to be careful. The team could live out the winter on Theo's thighs.

Coach Ernie Merrick calls us in for the team meeting. We watch selected video excerpts from the previous week's match, and the instruction to the attacking midfield players is to play the ball in behind the last defender. The video is paused and released, while Merrick and assistant coach Aaron Healey point to the patchwork of holes, the myriad of possibilities that open up as a team presses forward. I glance to my right, where gun new signing Leandro Love is sitting. He is Brazilian, with flair stamped all over him. I look at the dreads and a dazzling lobe-full of ear bling. He is being asked to do the team thing. I wonder whether Ernie would mind if I slip him a note that just reads "Go nuts, Leandro. Take 'em all on. You have a national stereotype to uphold."

In fact it's the Scottish-born Merrick who punches out a national stereotype, at the expense of the Auld country. "We don't sign full backs to kick in long balls. They play in Scotland, they don't play in Australia." The players giggle, because even after 30 years in his adopted country, Ernie has lost little of his accent. "Although Scotland just beat France on the weekend," he continues quickly, "so maybe the Scots are the new power in world football." The players drown him out with their bellowing. "I was wondering how long that would take to come out," Muscat laughs.

~

It's the job of media managers to sizzle with buzzwords and glow with smiles, but for Tony Ising, the Victory dream transcends mere occupation. The club quite literally was conceived on his notepad, his home computer during some dark moments at the end of 1997.

> It was the weekend immediately following Australia's elimina-
> tion from the World Cup to Iran, and at the next National
> Soccer League (NSL) match at Optus Oval, the place was like
> a morgue. Completely depressing. For mine, that was the
> darkest hour. But everyone around at that time finally saw that
> throwing all the eggs at the World Cup basket wasn't the
> answer, and that they really had to concentrate their efforts on
> making sure the national league stood on its own two feet.

Ising went home and wrote a rough business plan for a new club. He called it Melbourne Victory. He had no financial backers, nothing more than an idea and a vision for a new soccer team for Melbourne with a broad base of appeal. It was an idea before its time, because with moderate crowds and disappointing levels of sponsorship, the NSL was hardly looking for new teams. "The plan sat on the shelf for six years," Ising explains. "To enter a new team in the old league would have been commercial suicide."

But then along came Frank Lowy and a new start for Australian soccer. The A-League, modelled in part on the wildly successful Japanese J.League, was blueprinted, and suddenly, there was a need for teams. Ising dusted off his plan, and with help from News Limited executive Alen Rados, began knocking on doors. Eventually, Rados found a big name in Glenn Wheatley and deep pockets in the person of current Victory chairman Geoff Lord. The Victory had its name, its colours and, most importantly, its financial backer. The first person signed to the football department was not a player, but a football operations manager. Nearly three years later, Gary Cole, a Socceroos Hall of Famer who scored 20 times for his country, stands in the centre of Telstra Dome next to Merrick, a defender's bib slung over his torso, one which has thickened slightly since his playing days. "Is that a bib or a corset?" Ising jibes, drawing a two fingered salute from Cole. Incidentally, the two fingered salute is the signature of chairman Geoff Lord, offered to the audience at every corporate function, although he spins it around into an altogether more Churchillian V. I spoke to Cole after training, still corseted and beading with sweat.

> I'd given up. And my old football mates had given up. When it was announced that the NSL was dead and that there was going to be a rebirth, people of my generation said that this was the last roll of the dice. If the A-League doesn't work, then when is it ever going to work?

I ask Cole why it did work this time. Like most people, he credits the one team, one town philosophy, and also the absence of an ethnic stamp on the Victory.

> It's interesting because football's traditions in Australia are based in the ethnicity, and without it the sport could never have got to where it was. When I played for Heidelberg, I played in front of 15,000 people ... I'm so proud of playing for Heidelberg and Preston and those ethnic clubs, because they are the foundation, but the game couldn't go to where it is now. And anyone who doesn't see that has got his head in the sand.

Training concludes, and on the sidelines, two girls loudly proclaim that they are Rodrigo Vargas MySpace friends. "Are you going to the Chilean festival?" they squeal as their hero wanders over for some post-training photos. Vargas, the softly spoken son of a chicken proprietor at Queen Victoria market, confesses that he will miss the festival because he has a date with the Central Coast Mariners. I ask him whether he eats a lot of chicken. "Probably five nights a week," he says. "We love the chicken, springtime kangaroo, everything."

"You're a gun, Love," a group of five young fans yell in the direction of the new Brazilian signing. Daniel, Anthony, Joey, Joey, and Frankie; they're aged 11 to 13, and they've made their own way to the open training. Daniel screams "Archie! Archie!" as the team gathers at the fence. "Do you remember me from Socceroos training?"

"Of course I do, mate," Archie replies. The same congenial Archie who threw his boots into the crowd after every home game in the team's struggling first year. None of the hundred or so gathered fans leave without a signature from their favourite players. These are new local idols in an international game.

~

Kaz Patafta is 18 and has never worn this much make-up. He is on loan from Portuguese giant Benfica and a glossy photo shoot is still something of a novelty. "They tend to go for the Portuguese boys over there," he says.

I ask Patafta how he was recruited to the Victory. Archie Thompson answers for him. "Don't you know the story? Ernie was chatting up his missus."

The ability to lure a player of Patafta's ability back to Melbourne is one of Thompson's signposts that the game is getting healthier in Australia. I press him for the others. "Sitting down in a cinema and seeing a 90 second A-League ad; 50,000 people at a regular season match; 22,000 members for the Victory; and the Asian Champions League, which we've qualified for in 2008."

In the longer term, Thompson is also excited about the purpose-built football stadium in the Olympic Park precinct, and the recently mooted idea that Australia may bid to host a World Cup. "I love it when I'm driving and I see someone has a Melbourne Victory sticker on their car. I get excited about that. I also get excited when I see the number of people walking across the bridge and into Telstra Dome. It's just turning into something."

Skipper Kevin Muscat also feels the surge in momentum for his sport.

> For me the penny dropped when tickets went on sale for the (A-League) Grand Final. You're looking at 55,000 tickets, and it came on the radio that they were sold out in three hours. That's when it really struck home to me, that as a team and a code we'd made great strides.

Muscat is equally sure that this is not a passing fad, and that Melbourne is a genuine soccer town. That realisation was etched in stone on the night he scored the winner at the MCG against Uruguay in 2001.

> We'd won the match and it was 2.30 in the morning. I was with Craig Moore and we couldn't sleep, so we went for a walk. We got to the food court at the casino, and turned the corner, and as we walked through, the whole food court stood up and gave us a standing ovation. I'd never seen the sport get recognition before, but they just all stood up and clapped. And that made me realise that if we got our act together as a code, there were opportunities.

The photographer calls Muscat in front of the lens. "Put your hands behind your back, Kevin, put pressure on your hip. We'll do this. Then we'll do some laughing." He snaps away, and then finishes with a series where the captain has a ball for a head. Muscat jokes that these are the best ones, the ones where he has no face. I quietly wonder if the photographer knows Kevin Muscat, has seen him play. I think about offering some advice. Play the safe route. Include Kevin's face.

~

The theatrically named Hamlet Armenian scores the first goal for the Whittlesea Zebras against Green Gully and a dozen dancing youths light up Bob Jane Stadium with song. "Hamlet Arm-en-ian, Hamlet Arm-en-ian."

The tune is operatic and I should know it, although years of television watching has reduced it to just "that Leggo's ad". Hamlet himself sprints joyously towards his supporter group, and I pray that as part of his celebration he will raise a human skull aloft. To score, perchance to dream. Whittlesea, in its Juventus strip, flies its ethnic colours proudly. Its opponent in this final, Green Gully, is historically tied to the Maltese community. Indeed most of the Victorian Premier League (VPL) clubs are linked, at least historically, to an ethnic community.

I'm watching the game with Ian Syson, a football fan and writer, and the founder of Libero Press, Australia's first exclusively football publishing house. It would be wrong to call Syson a Victory hater—he has attended, after all, nearly every home game—but his first love is the VPL and, in particular, South Melbourne, formerly South Melbourne Hellas. Syson clings to a shrinking hope that South may be admitted to the A-League as a second Melbourne-based team.

> The biggest problem for football under the old structure was corruption at upper levels. I think Soccer Australia was a basket case for a very long time, and the game was never going to get anywhere until changes were made. But I think the new FFA has thrown the baby out with the bathwater with this policy of non-ethnic teams.

I mention to Syson that almost everyone in the city would disagree with him, given the Victory's popularity and the success of the "one city, one team" policy. Syson nods ruefully.

I think the A-League is missing a lot of people who don't go from some clubs in Melbourne because they feel that the process of ethnic cleansing hurt them. Hurt their history. Hurt their club. South Melbourne is the most successful club in the history of Australian football, and yet was told, "need not apply". Whether that decision was right or wrong, and I think it was wrong, you can see why people were hurt by the A-League ... What would have happened if we had that World Cup success and the NSL had still been happening? What would have happened to the NSL?

The debate around ethnicity centres on violence, and whether football under the old NSL structure was a lightning rod for ethnic clashes. Syson says that he has seen over 80 South games at Bob Jane Stadium, and only twice has he seen punches thrown, although he did miss a particularly controversial South versus Preston game. He is convinced that violence at soccer matches is grossly over-reported. "Soccer was always the game that threatened the comfortable hegemony of Australian sport. If soccer gets anywhere, it starts to eat into rugby league and it starts to eat into Australian rules. So there's a vested interest in linking ethnic disaffection with soccer."

For his Das Libero website, Syson is researching the way crowd violence is reported. It's his theory that the drunken cricket lout is characterised as an isolated idiot, but the drunken soccer lout is immediately an ultra-nationalist.

"I'm not an apologist for people pursuing their nationalist agendas," Syson concludes. "At the pre-season practice match (between South and Victory) the actions of a couple of so-called South supporters sickened me. But I do want to make sure people know what we're talking about when we say violence. That we're comparing apples with apples."

In extra time, Whittlesea's Steve Martin taps home the winner, and the majority of the 700-odd fans go wild.

"Two one to the Whittlesea" sing the vocal Zebras supporter group celebrating behind the goal, before rounding out with an a cappella version of "Seven Nation Army". They are the FDZ, and they laughingly describe themselves as "ultras" because the 12 of them are being guarded by two security guards.

Jason, a Whittlesea local, says the Zebras are his number one passion. "I've been following them for eight years, and that's where my heart lies. I'm in the minority though. These boys prefer the Victory. They watch the Zebras to have an interest in the off-season." I ask Jason whether a club like South Melbourne should be admitted to the A-League. "I would," he says. "You can't make another plastic club. There are rumours of the Gold Coast Galaxy ... for heaven's sake ..."

The final whistle blows, and after a brief celebration, there's a collective rush for the tram to take us to the Victory game. I'm running with Ian Syson and his 10-year-old son, Dan. We make the tram, and Dan removes his blue and white South Melbourne shirt and replaces it with the navy, white and silver of the Victory. His father smiles. "He might wear that, but you still want to play for South, don't you, Dan?"

~

"We're north end, we're north end, we're north end over here." The north terrace fans sing this song every home game, and the south terrace answers, like birds answering the call of a mate. One of the lovely quirks of this tradition is that it was established at Olympic Park, where the north terrace fans actually sat at the northern end. At Telstra Dome, they sit at the southern or Coventry end. Nevertheless, the ritual continues, unadjusted: the north terrace fans declaring their northness from the south. The south terrace fans declaring their southness from the north.

The Victory is in the middle of a home goal drought, and it doesn't break against Central Coast. It isn't a bad game though, and the team has a flush of chances in the last 10 minutes. When the final whistle blows we are out of our seats. If Thompson hadn't been brought down deliberately in the last few minutes, he would have been clean through, one-on-one with the keeper. The lower-level retractable seating shakes with the injustice of it all. Rita Zammit, who travelled with me to Germany last year, is red with excitement. "This is what football is about, frustration, disappointment, excitement. I mean the adrenaline was pumping, even if there was no score ... The state of football? There were 27,000 people here on a Sunday night. Where would we have been three years ago?"

Archie Thompson walks slowly towards us and kicks a ball into the crowd. A kid called Anthony, 12, who has "Go Archie" painted on his cheeks, tells the same story with his lungs. Rita swoons in adoration:

> If you ask people in Melbourne who you know in football, it's no longer Neill or Bresciano, it's Archie Thompson. I mean you ask the kids. It's Archie this, Archie that. That's a big step. We finally have a local face of football in this town, and his name is Archie Thompson. We've come a long way.

Lifestyle

CHARLES FIRTH

A hookworm's-eye view of the world around us

I was in Pyongyang last week and, boy, are those guys paranoid. I was there in the days after the South Korean President, Roh Moo-hyun, took his historic trip across the 38th parallel. You'd think that would make them more relaxed about technically still being at war with the greatest military superpower in world history. And yet they still think the United States is about to attack them.

Ridiculous. When was the last time the United States attacked a small nation just because they had some sort of program for the development of weapons of mass destruction floating around? Oh.

The difference this time is, of course, that North Korea has proven it has WMD, which kind of makes the diplomacy a bit different. Apparently the United States has taken to using words such as "respect" and "dialogue" rather than "bomb you back to" and "the Stone Age".

One night I was sitting at the bar of Hotel Pyongyang where the beers are 50 cents a longneck (if you're looking for a great holiday I recommend North Korea—go with a humanitarian pretext, stay for the command economy). Anyway, I got chatting to a suave, grey-sweatered, long-faced guy from the foreign ministry who coolly told me in impeccable English that relations between the United States and North Korea were like "the tiger and the hedgehog".

At first I thought he had simply had too many 50-cent long-necks, but the more he explained the more he made sense. When the tiger tries to bite the hedgehog, it gets stuck in the tiger's mouth, and the spikes get stuck in the tiger's nose. As he explained this, he chewed on a stinky yellow strip of fish jerky—a delicacy that was stuck in the mouth of everyone at the bar: eight years of famine drives people to do some pretty horrifying stuff.

Being stuck in the tiger's mouth, though, is where North Korea wants to be. This means that even though the hedgehog is very small, he can control the direction the tiger heads in. "Hedgehogs are small but prickly," concluded the man with a smug grin that made me think for a moment he was a French diplomat, even though he was short and Asian.

Having discovered the essence of North Korea's foreign policy (deep background research in North Korea is amazingly cheap—the whole conversation only cost me $3.50—even including the jerky, which had me "researching" Pyongyang's plumbing systems for the rest of the night), it got me thinking. If America is the tiger and North Korea is a hedgehog, where does Australia fit in?

A few days later, I was hanging out with a former Chinese military spy in Tiananmen Square (it's a long story—but it ended with us being detained by police, of course). He started telling me about how he perceives China's role in the world. "It's like the tiger and the snake," he said. Apparently, China is the snake—you can beat it with a stick, you can chop off its tail and it won't die. And yet it can kill with just one bite which the tiger won't even have seen coming.

All this talk got me feeling sorry for tigers—after all, our success in the world is directly tied to the United States. Like it or not, Australia's future does not bode well if our friend the tiger is limping around with a hedgehog in its mouth.

So what exactly is Australia in this overly extended metaphor? I'd like to think Australia is a kookaburra, sitting high up on a distant tree, laughing at the rest of the animals. Others would prefer us to be a koala, sitting in the tree, stoned, not paying much attention to the world around us. But the truth is slightly less fun. If China is a snake, North Korea is a hedgehog and the United States is a tiger, then Australia is the hookworm of the world. It has penetrated the skin of the tiger and is making a decent living in its lower intestine. But it depends on the tiger's survival to ensure its own survival.

Which is probably why I favour eating fish jerky, and using diplomatic words with the hedgehogs. It beats having our host run around with spikes up its nose.

STEVE VIZARD

The Library hotel, Thailand, and other hip hotels

"Hip is the sophistication of the wise primitive in a giant jungle", Norman Mailer provocatively proclaimed in his 1957 essay "The White Negro", between stabbing his second wife and collecting a Pulitzer Prize. If Mailer had been poolside last week at Thailand's hippest hotel, the Library, I'm fairly confident he would have stabbed my 13-year-old son Jim. And he wouldn't have been alone.

The Library is a phalanx of cubes clustered around a glass library in the form of another cube overlooking the best bit of Koh Samui's perfect beach. It doesn't need a copy of Mailer's book on its shelves to exude hip. A triumph of right angles. Interiors by Euclid. Lines so sharp you can disembowel yourself leaning against a door-frame. Monochrome décor. Black benches. White, enamel-painted floorboards. Black stools. White matte walls. Staying at the Library is like vacationing on a chessboard. If Boris Spassky and Annie Lennox had a love child and it was a building, this is what it would look like—a minimalist structure so architecturally pure that even checking in creates clutter.

At least that's what happens when we check in. You can almost see the only other visible guests—the Argentine supermodel couple and a cigar-chewing Italian Marlon Brando circa *Godfather*—start packing and changing flights. The Library isn't expecting our family. Or any family. And it certainly isn't expecting 13-year-old Jim. Within minutes Jim is dismembering hipness: Jim emptying contents of bar fridge; Jim locating iMac in library; Jim download-ing dance tracks at blaringly loud levels; Jim ringing room service; Jim befriending eleven local Thai boys and instigating international soccer match using as goalpost a chaise-longue-bearing, cigar-gnawing Mafia guy; Jim feeding entire soccer team and their distant relatives on room service; Jim purchasing incendiary device in the form of skyrocket from Thai pedlar on beach; series of ex-plosions outside Argentine supermodel bedroom; Jim unavailable for comment.

Jim is wild but this joint is wilder.

Our bedroom is a giant white box as vast as Mailer's ego. On one side, raised on a rostrum, is a double bed. At the other end is a bath. It might be a bath. It's hard to distinguish its white silhouette against the white walls in a white room, which strangely evoke the sense of skiing and après skiing simultaneously. The Library lives and breathes the hip dictum, form over function. No cupboards. No wardrobes. No racks. Only white surfaces. I spend twenty min-utes feeling the walls looking for concealed storage cavities. The cleaners who valiantly attempt to make sense of my daily pigsty are equally hamstrung by lack of storage. Their solution is to repack my clothes into my suitcase each day. For an establishment that markets itself as "a leader in Thai hospitality", there is nothing less hospitable than finding one's suitcases packed every day. The hotel is screaming, Get the hell out of here. Take your battered suitcase with your soiled underwear and your fake Polo shirt and the pre-posterous crumpled reefer jacket you brought to the tropics on the off chance of a formal dinner and your hyperactive son and his pirated DVDs and get the hell out of our brochure.

Outside, in the Library's obsessively manicured gardens, Queen's Bishop Two to King's Pawn Three, the dominating land-scaping feature is a vast square red mosaic pool. Bright red. Every time I wade in I feel like I'm bleeding from the ankles. When Jim and his eleven mates relocate their soccer match to the pool, the overall scene resembles the first twenty minutes of *Saving Private Ryan*. On the pool's edge, a lank-haired photographer and his lank-haired offsider man an expensive-looking Minolta on a tripod. Twice I walk or swim in their general direction, and twice the photographic duo abandons their post as if a solar eclipse has consumed the light. It isn't just that I am getting in the road of their shoot; reality is getting in the road. I watch them. Extreme close-up of foot of chair. Extreme close-up of prawn on plate. Extreme close-up of fork prong. An extreme close-up of lard-assed, middle-aged Australian cavorting in red water, in a manner reminiscent of dying mammal on the upper deck of a Japanese whaler, is never on the cards. Neither is any image capturing any human being.

The Library, like all hip hotels, lives in extreme close-up. It is a *Wallpaper* shoot. It is a freeze frame. It is best viewed through a macro lens, the better to magnify particulars, to distort reality, to render everyday life as a pastiche, too close, too far away, too hard, too soft, never just right.

~

In downtown Munich, Bavaria, the City Hilton is the black hole of hipness.

"Have you got one of our Hilton family cards so you can stay anywhere in our portfolio of over three thousand branded hotels in the global marketplace?" recites the well-groomed Hilton beauty in the grey Hilton uniform presiding over the grey counter. I can't place her accent. She could be from anywhere. So could the Munich City Hilton.

"The card guarantees you'll feel at home no matter where your travels take you."

There it is. She said it. "Feel at home." Hilton hotels, chain hotels, comfort hotels, airport hotels, family hotels, the lot of them, all of them aim to minimise disruption and replicate your known universe. Conformity is king. It's in their strategic plans. Millions of bulk-buy chocolates on millions of synthetic pillows across every continent are daily reminders that hidden teams are working round the clock to make you feel like you are somewhere else. The same somewhere else. Not here. Your place, not ours. Home.

Hip hotels are home wreckers. Hip hotels despise your known universe, maximise disruption, transport you nowhere. Nowhere else matters. Nowhere else exists. "They've got three thousand hotels; Hell, we've got one. They've got five million rooms; Hell, we've got twelve. And we're thinking of getting rid of them." I suspect the hippest hotel in the world has no rooms. Merely a lobby and chandeliers and a bevy of Calvin Klein bellhops in black T-shirts wearing Blutooth earpieces, talking to no one and carting luggage nowhere. Check in to our dream on our terms. Here is the key card to our existentialist abode; welcome to the narcissism of our "enormous present", take it or leave it.

"Uniquely memorable experience" is the defining characteristic of the hip hotel, conclude the hip hotel guides. Perhaps. But not entirely. Holidaying in a caravan at Rosebud with my Uncle Frank and Aunt Carol and two incontinent cocker spaniels is a uniquely memorable experience. Twelve years in a gulag is a uniquely memorable experience. Unique and memorable might be necessary conditions but there's more.

Hip hotels tease: they draw you in and spit you out. They flaunt themselves like upmarket Russian hookers, splendid in their designer labels and scarlet lipsticks, half-buttoned skirts, glimpses of thighs, mirror black shoes, all come-on and procuration, yet ultimately unprocurable. There are names for women like these hotels. And for a moment, a split second, you consider that this might be, could in the right circumstances be the perfect place, that the rest of life should resemble this space. In truth, you know this is a one-night stand with calculated lunacy. Angelina Jolie with rooms.

Take the Portobello Hotel in London's Notting Hill: another sort of hip again, as different as David Bowie's irises, yet still mesmerically hip. The Portobello. Velvet, bric-a-brac, chandeliers, clusters of worn couches, shabby chic hip, an antique bulk lot from the Sunday market, both cool and chaotic simultaneously. Two former inner-city terrace houses are somehow connected by mazes of servant staircases. The Portobello has the sense of an Escher print. Staircases that seemingly take you from your bedroom lead you back again. Hogswood on Amex.

On the other side of Piccadilly, the "surreal Cocteau-like atmosphere" of the Sanderson delivers another strain of hip courtesy of Philippe Starck. The foyer houses a giant pair of Dali lips as a couch. That's it. Pretty much just a pair of lips in a tundra of a vestibule. Arriving at the Sanderson is like checking in to Mick Jagger's head. A maze of floor to ceiling translucent sheer curtains hang on a network of rails creating the impression of a tram terminus on the roof. I arranged to meet my business associate Shaun in the curtained spaces. I knew he was in there somewhere. I could see shapes and shadows. I could hear his asthmatic wheeze. Someone was moving. My search through the curtains, chasing ghosts and the slap of leather footsteps, turned out to be less of a meeting and more of a psychological thriller.

The Library. The Sanderson. The Portobello. The Bulgari. The Mondrian. There are no common master plans here, only individual tales of eccentricity and obsession.

Hipness is a thief, appropriating stuff from everywhere, prowling back lane dumpsters and suburban housing estates and op shops for the next big thing. Everything's up for recycling. Anything. Take my grandma. Grandma's three-bedroom brick-veneer house, the one she's lived in for the past forty years, is a hip hotel in waiting.

Complimentary mug of Milo and a homemade orange cake on arrival. The talking budgies and the cuttlefish bells. The '50s floral retro couches and a set of ceramic ducks taking off from the wall-papered lounge room. A level of service that borders on obsessive albeit a tad slow. Fluffy purple acrylic toilet seat covers. Shabby chic so chic it's all shabby. I can see the brochure. Extreme close-up of a knitted toilet roll cover. Extreme close-up of a homemade pasty. Name? I'm thinking something like "The Frame". Or "Mothballs". Or "Terminus".

In this Galapagos of narcissism, the designer is king. Ludwig of Bavaria would have made a fantastic hip hotel owner. Walt Disney, too, had the perfect temperament, with particular reference to creating a talking mouse/steamboat captain and cryogenically freezing his own head. All four of Walt's twisted kingdoms proclaim the magnetism of designer insanity.

And Mailer. Mailer's work mythologised everything around him, just as Mailer's life mythologised Mailer. Mailer spent a life romanticising. It was all about him, as over-inflated and caricatured and attention-grabbing as an inflatable jumping castle. Less hotel, more hip. More him. That's the point of hip hotels. Audience, statement, me.

~

Madison Avenue was always going to pounce on the hip hotel. Just as it pounced on hip. Charlie Parker was dead but his soul was ripe for the picking, The Bird's plaintive wailings made cool for the masses, commercialised from a downtown jazz club to a billion home stereos. Hip is the mass marketer's R&D department.

The cool madness of the hip hotel was perfect for the mass marketers. They knew they could spin a story about place and belonging. In an age of confusion we thirst for meaning. In an age where we stumble through virtual worlds and sprawling shopping malls, we crave identity. The hip hotel stands for something, says something, proclaims its identity for all to see. It's implicit in the Library marketing material and I'm a sucker for it. Our world is a world of red pools and shimmering drapes. For a day or a week, you can share in our precocious dream, walk in our absurdity. Be mad. Be eccentric. Be noticed. Be different. Be something. Be hip.

Check out the bar fridges, a cacophony of weird merchandising. Chocolate frogs and boxes of herbs. Swimming goggles and multivitamin tablets and toolkits. At the Como in Melbourne, yellow rubber ducks. At the Mondrian in Los Angeles, pencils, pencils everywhere—on pillows, on the bar fridge, by the bed and in bathrooms.

"Shoppers get the chance for total immersion", declares the definitive German guidebook to designer hotels. Fashion brands and fashion designers are now claiming the domain of the hip hotel and I'm scared. What common skill base connects a belt and a bedroom? Mont Blanc make great pens, but I have no desire to be immersed in a restaurant created by a design team whose principal preoccupation hitherto has been whether a tiny white knob at the end of a writing instrument should swivel clockwise or anticlockwise. Total immersion is worthy, provided one is immersed in the right thing.

The Continentale in Florence is so perfectly immersed in itself it demands ransacking. Michele Bonan's version of heaven, its "femme pastel pop art interiors" are asking for a full frontal assault by skyrockets and a teenage soccer team. Here at full rack rate is the solipsism of designers playing at being designers, a seductive hybrid of accommodation and display case that simulates sleeping in the front window of Harvey Nichols. Here the pink velvet knob is turned to eleven. The Continentale is fashion week with mattresses and key cards and the only item missing from the bedroom is a cash register.

The Continentale "world of Ferragamo" needs to meet my world of Jim and five kids and birthday parties and chocolate cakes and a rampaging terrier and then let's see how spotlessly their white translucent sheers hang. I want Jim to bust up the place. I want to hurl my sweaty no-brand singlet over the Murano chandelier. I want to sprawl over the Minotti chaise longue quaffing meat pies, spilling sauce on the zebrano timber, my sweaty feet all over the Colefax and Fowler wallpaper, watching football at full blare, annoying neighbours. I want to wallow. Walk in my shoes for a day and let's see you survive the mortar attacks of my world: of discarded ring pulls, tossed peanut packets and spilt salt that spreads like dandruff over the charcoal pile and grey-inked fingerprints of yesterday's newspapers all over your white hand-stitched leather and crinkled shopping bags and blunt plastic razors and wet towels and five-day-old socks. Let's see how you deal with the flotsam of my life.

~

By the time I arrive in Mailer's metropolis, forty years and twenty blocks away, New York's original hip hotel, Morgans, is history. She is a 50-year-old supermodel intent on walking the red carpet and all I can see are crow's-feet and sunspots and I don't want to know. The once hip basement bar is now a basement with a bar in it, and no offer of free pencils or rubber ducks can wallpaper over the cracks or summon up the glory days. In a city of twenty million, in this city of twenty million, birthplace of Warhol and Blue Note, you don't expect everyone at this hotel to be hip. Just someone. And at Morgans' prices, one of them is supposed to be me. The time had come and gone for Morgans.

Ammianus Marcellinus, a fourth-century Bill Bryson, chronicled the decaying days of the Roman empire with the all-seeing eye of an early Michelin inspector:

> Those few mansions, which were once celebrated for the serious
> cultivation of liberal studies, now are filled with ridiculous

amusements of torpid indolence, reechoing with the sound of singing, and the tinkle of flutes and lyres. You find a singer instead of a philosopher; a teacher of silly arts is summoned in place of an orator, the libraries are shut up like tombs, organs played by waterpower are built, and lyres so big that they look like wagons! and flutes, and huge machines suitable for the theater.

Marcellinus arrived at his accommodation on the Palatino too late, nearly four centuries too late, to witness real Roman hip, proving that hip and square are flip sides of the same denarius, separated by the razor thin enemy of all that is cool—time. Hip is not merely how one looks at the uber objet, but when. If the hippest guesthouse in Heidelberg, Zum Güldenen Schaf, had decorated its walls with truckloads of gilt buddhas and Che Gueverra portraits a century prematurely in 1891, local pedagogue Gottlob Frege might well have observed of it, hip at evening and square by morning.

Hip is as time-sensitive as a soufflé. Too early, it's a treacly novelty. Too late, it's as indigestible as Cliff Richard unplugged.

I invariably arrive too early. Or too late. The enemy of the hip hotel is me. People just like me. And Jim. When suits with briefcases and kids with iPods check in, hipness checks out. Herein lies the Library's trick, the hip marketer's triumphant sleight of hand, the fundamental audacity of the hip hotel: the hip hotel welcomes the customer to the dream never disclosing that the dreamer has left the building. It leaves the customer alone to fill the gaps, to connect the dots, to create the backstory. To insert life. For one night only, for the price of a bed, the unwitting latecomer customer plays at being the designer; the audience plays at being the hipster never suspecting he's paying top dollar for a stale vision of paradise and his own handiwork.

And that's the paradox of hipness. Hip has rooms to fill, but despises a full house. Hip stands apart but chases its own tail.

Today's shocking pink interiors at Philip Treacy's laughingly hip hotel the g in Galway are tomorrow's suburban housing estate, back whence they came, ashes to ashes.

Mailer knew the transience of hip. Even as he uttered it, Mailer was checking out and moving on, fuelled by his own unspoken revelation that the ultimate destination is never the hip of this moment, but the electric anticipation of the next.

GERMAINE GREER

Who cares if she can't sing and can't dance? Posh Spice is the Damien Hirst of dress-wearing

I have said very mean things about Victoria Beckham in my time, such as that she could neither dance nor sing and should give up her disastrous efforts at a solo career while she and David had some money left. I take none of them back. What I have lately come to realise is that what Victoria understands is clothes. She knows what to wear and she knows how to wear it. The revelation came in the form of an unforgettable pink dress.

The Moon dress by Roland Mouret that Victoria wore when she attended the press conference that welcomed her husband to LA Galaxy last summer is a work of genius. Mouret's designs usually begin with draping a model in fabric, in this case, 96% cotton and 4% elastane. By making two double-sided folds from nipple to neckline he constructed a bodice with oblique side-seams joining extended cap-sleeves that stand proud of the shoulders, each stiffened by another small origami fold. The front panel is divided by an inch-wide half-belt that holds one edge of a folded tab into which two more folds are set. The straight skirt ends at mid-knee. Some sources claim that the back zipper extends from nape to hem, which would mean that you can walk into the dress like a cupboard, but this impression appears mistaken. Victoria's dress that day had a kickpleat at the back.

As Victoria would tell you herself, it is the extra half-inch that counts, but nearly all the women who have worn the real dress have given in to the temptation to wear it a size too small. Not Victoria. As she prowled along the hot green turf of the playing field, the perfect background colour for the cold pink of the dress, the half-belt sat flat on her natural waist and the skirt moved easily. Off the peg, the Moon dress would set you back about £1,000. By teaming it with a matching pink ostrich-skin Birkin bag by Hermès and hoisting herself five inches higher on stupendous Balenciaga heels, with no added tat, no bling, no gloves, no hat, Victoria did that clever, innovative dress proud.

On GMTV last Thursday, Kate Garraway wore a knock-off of the Mouret Moon dress. Several such knock-offs are doing the rounds; this one was near-enough a replica and all wrong. Next to the red sofa, the pink turned puce. The dress was so much too small that small puffs of flesh extruded at each armhole. The cap sleeves were too meagre to begin with and, because the dress was too tight, they sat too close into the neck, thereby overemphasising the bust, and that was before Garraway decided to clutter the neckline with a bulky necklace. The side-view was a disaster, every bulge mercilessly outlined. Real elegance requires not only a great dress, but a discriminating and disciplined wearer. Suddenly I was reckoning Victoria Beckham among the all-time greats, alongside Wallis Simpson and Coco Chanel. She could make Anna Wintour look dowdy.

It must have been Victoria Beckham who sold the idea of managing Mouret to Simon Fuller, who parlayed the Spice Girls to their success, and has continued to manage her and David Beckham ever since. When Mouret showed his first collection at London Fashion Week in 1998, he was the property of Sharai and Andre Meyers, who had 100% of the label. In 2005, he was named red carpet designer of the year at the British Fashion Awards. His Galaxy dress, with its square neckline and draped shoulders, was the must-have of 2005; Scarlett Johansson, Beyonce, Nicole Kidman, Rachel Weisz and Keira Knightley were all photographed wearing it more and less well. In October 2005, Mouret dissociated himself from the Meyerses, leaving them holding the name Roland Mouret Designs and nothing else, and gave himself extended sick leave. His next dress, the Titanium, was so eagerly awaited that to get one you had to put your name down, wait for months, and save up £950.

When the Mouret label was relaunched in 2007 as 19RM, in homage to Fuller's 19 Entertainment, Mrs Beckham bought all 21 items in the collection, for a mere £30,000 or so, the price of three of her Hermès Birkin handbags. She had probably already decided to wear the Moon dress for her appearance at LA Galaxy four months before it would be available in any department store. Because it would be seen in sunlight and therefore in its true hue, she chose orchid pink, an unusual colour for her. Ordinary mortals could buy the dress in black, white or navy; only Bergdorf Goodman in New York would ever carry the pink. In darker colours, the architecture of the dress is difficult to appreciate; in pink, every fold counted.

Victoria Beckham may have seemed the least talented of the Spice Girls but her real talent lay elsewhere. She is an artist in the same genre as Damien Hirst: marketing. In an era of bare bellies, painted legs, visible underwear, junk jewellery and grisly computer generated prints, she is a lone champion of elegance for working girls. In an endorsement for the paperback edition of her book, *That Extra Half an Inch*, Mouret credits her with making "high fashion relevant for everyone". So why does she always pout? Why doesn't she ever smile? I reckon it's because she knows that when she smiles, she looks like a chipmunk. Anyway, grinning isn't glamorous.

PETER LALOR

Fashion pinkoes are the fifth columnists of masculinity

A male colleague asked if I thought his shirt was a disgrace. I had no qualms telling him it was. I said the shirt in question was worse than a disgrace, it was a crime. Genocide, no less.

I followed up with a long dissertation on why a man in Barbie doll pink was an affront to both nature and nurture, a gesture of surrender that will one day see us sitting down to urinate and ringing each other to see what we'll be wearing out on Friday night.

There may have been some mention that the great gods of masculinity did not fight the long war for this. Would Johnny Cash be considered one of the greatest entertainers if he had wandered squinting into the Nashville footlights, curled his lip and announced: "I'm the man in pink"?

Would masters of the ancient Asiatic assassin cults aspire to homicidal greatness if they were to bow before their master and be presented with a lovely pink belt?

Would the Rolling Stones have pulled off all that satanic majesty make-over that so successfully wedged the Beatles had they sung "Paint it Pink"?

"Hell man," I cried:

Your shirt might get you accepted at a seven-year-old's fairy party but it ain't gonna cut it at the inner circle of my darkness. You have insulted our noble DNA, torn up the colour code chart of honour that sets us apart from the hordes who believe things get better when you talk about them.

And, don't call me unreconstructed. I have renovated. I have no problem with men who lie with other men, men who choose to watch a hanky-soaking drama instead of sport, men who have no difficulty remembering their wives' birthdays or their children's names. But a man who wears pink is beyond the pale.

Apparently I had missed the point. The chap in question meekly informed me he was not asking my opinion about the colour of his shirt, but the collar of his shirt.

The chap's collar was torn and he was uncertain whether this was acceptable.

I wiped the spit from my chin and his face and put a masculine arm around his brotherly shoulder. "Don't worry," I said. "I have a needle and thread in my man bag and we'll have you looking tickety boo in a minute or two."

I'm starting to realise the battle against pink is lost, but before I let go I want to relate the experience of another colleague who was playing pool against a rough-looking chap in a pub.

The straight-talking builder-type grabbed my significantly less masculine mate's pink shirt in his callused fingers and asked "did it get mixed up with the red socks mate?"

I blame television. And Kerry Packer. There was a time when everything beamed into our lounge rooms came in shades ranging from black to white.

The apartheid broadcasting era ended sometime around the time of Lillee and Thommo and before you could say "Graham Kennedy has a rather effeminate approach to colour coding" Packer's band of privatised cricketers were putting their creams in the wash with every sock colour you can imagine. The poor old Windies suffered the humiliation of being forced to wear pink during the early stages of the competition.

When I was at uni the smart kids used to talk about form influencing content or some such. I often wondered, as I served these scholars their cheese toast and cleaned their tables, what they were talking about. Now I think I get it.

Form influencing content is, like, when the television itself changes what's on the television. So when colour telly came in, cricketers started wearing coloured clothes.

Which got me thinking about the rash of programs on television concentrating on generous arses. For a while everything on the bloody box had to do with overweight and sweaty people wearing lycra. You saw fat people running, fat people in the gym, fat people on bikes and fat people abseiling. There were lots of shots of fat people in slow motion. Fat looks good in slow motion. There's more drama. It goes up, slowly. Then—wait for it—it goes down. Slowly.

I had wondered what was going on and realised it was the wide screen TV. I wonder if it is a case of the (fried) chicken or the (fried) egg. What came first? Did television manufacturers build the wide screen because we're all getting fatter or did we get fatter because of wide screen?

Another blokey colleague has just arrived at my desk asking if his arse looks big in the new suit he's bought.

JOHN LETHLEAN

Silence of the lamb

"We're getting a lamb?" asked big ears with touching excitement. "Yes," I replied, "but I don't think it'll look much like what you've got in mind."

Took it pretty well, I thought, given the explanation that this lamb—this whole lamb—was coming to dinner as guest of honour. I had a full head of steam about this animal and it was riding roughshod over a 10-year-old's sensibilities.

It's easy to get carried away with the whole romantic pure-produce/first principles idea. And in the abstract, a whole milk-fed lamb is a notion to nourish all manner of needs if your idea of great food is gnarly bits of meat, cooked simply with oodles of flavour; low on glamour, high on satisfaction. The whole Slow Food/do it yourself/massage it with love thing.

But concept and reality can take divergent courses.

The background? I was on the phone to smallgoods entrepreneur Andrew Vourvahakis, a man all pigs fear this time of year, discussing the specifications for the yuletide leg of porcine bliss—the ham order is an important conversation—when he said something about milk-fed lambs from Flinders Island.

Supplying a few restaurants, he said. Good product.

It must have been cold; the weather has a profound influence on what I'm thinking about eating. While the season was undoubtedly heading towards fish and salads, I started thinking about warming winter braises and red meat.

"Whole milk-fed lambs, eh Andrew?"

It was meant to be a thought bubble; what would I, a bloke who can barely joint a chicken, do with a whole mammal? However, I must have articulated some kind of moaning desire, or maybe it was a dodgy phone line, because the next week in a bright-red Andrew's Choice box arrived a lamb. Pretty much the whole beast.

I was excited. In the cryovac bag, in two separate pieces, were the rump/legs and the balance of the torso, dressed (I think that's the correct expression for a carcass that's ready to "break down").

I cleaned out a shelf of the beer fridge, pushed lamby in tight and … Cripes! What next?

Excitement turned to trepidation. Was I really going to take my first butchery practical on this valuable carcass? Would I follow pictures in books, which belongs in the same category as making sense of architect's drawings?

I turned up the boost on the fridge and waited for fate to intervene, which he/she did about three days later when I asked a chef I was chatting to—Dwayne Bourke, from The Argo, a man good at all this primal stuff—what I should do with my lamb.

"Depends on what you want to cook, I suppose," came his answer. It couldn't be argued. But it didn't get me any closer to doing something useful with my little sheep.

Then, like the voice of salvation itself, I heard the words: "Why don't you bring it over and I'll bone it out for you and re-cryovac it in a few different bags?"

Hallelujah.

By the time I got to Bourke's kitchen towing the long-wheelbase Esky a few days later, I knew I wanted to make a wet roast—

abbacchio alla romana—for a boys' weekend (nice change from the barbecue)—and maybe keep at least one leg for roasting, but the rest ...

"Good meat," he said as he flicked his special knife around bones in a manner that suggested experience. It was pale and sweet-smelling. In the time it took for me to drink a coffee, we had the meat from two shoulders/forelegs/necks expertly removed from the bones in two separate pieces, two once conjoined legs ready for roasting and two loins with belly flaps for filling and rolling and roasting. And a lot of bones for the old dog (yes, I know you don't give uncooked bones to a dog, but believe me, it won't be a brittle shoulder that takes a 15-year-old arthritic lab from this earth).

In the end, one of the legs had to be seconded to the abbacchio to get the quantity up for eight would-be surfers; it's one of those chuck-it-all in a pan kind of dishes—lamb, wine, stock, herbs, aromatics, tomatoes—that you finish with breadcrumbs and Parmigiano. I chucked in some anchovy, too: not in the recipe, but what the hell. Very straightforward, and if I do say so myself, bloody great. We had it with polenta and artichokes out of my garden; my best impersonation yet of the mature, 30-something Jamie Oliver (allowing for the rather obvious age difference).

With a lot of vino and the latest *RocKwiz* trivia book, a great night of male bonding was had. And, having watched my chef, I feel ready to tackle the task personally next time a might-have-been-a-sheep comes a-knocking.

Santa, I need a boning knife for Christmas. And no, son, we are not getting a lamb for the backyard. The only small ruminant I want to see round here is silent. Very.

JOHN LETHLEAN

Telly tubbies

It was a day like any other really. With one serious exception.

Instead of getting up, doing all the usual stuff and skulking off to the workstation, I got up early, went straight to the couch and watched television, all day.

I was crook; I'd loved to have blamed the flu vaccination but in fact I was poorly before the nice nurse did her jabbing. Next day, I switched on and rostered myself off. Nobody was home to feel sorry for me, but that didn't seem a reason not to wallow in self-pity on their behalf. And what's the point of paying for subscription television if you don't exploit it?

So, instead of hitting the keyboard, I slipped into a sleeping bag, grabbed a pillow and hit the three-seater. And watched the food channel. All day.

At 6am, on comes Michael Chiarello's *Napa*. Never heard of it. Or him. I'm drinking orange juice and Chinese tea; he's stuffing a leg of pork with onions and spices. He's slick, confident, gregarious. He's American, for goodness sake. He looks like a Gap model and I even like the food he's doing. I hate him.

Next is Georges Laurier, from Quebec, in *Cook Like a Chef*. It's another glam cooking demo with more raw meat, a bit much at this hour really. He exhibits all the traits of his predecessor, except he's wearing chef's whites, not Gap.

"Reez-oh-toe, what a nice dish," says Georges as he demonstrates the 1235th risotto technique ever done on telly. No wonder I can't make risotto.

Top Chef accompanies sunrise. It's a reality elimination game for aspiring chefs, nine hyped-up Americans whose first challenge is to cook a dish based on ingredients bought for $20 at a petrol station. Intense. But strangely compelling. The product placement is shameless.

Cooking in Paradise: Gioconda Scott speaks Spanish better than she cooks for a camera, but nothing surpasses her Oxbridge vowels. Coxon's *Royal Feast*: everything you didn't need to know about the cooking of a royal family in South Africa. Yawn. *Party Starters*. American tripe.

Time for some toast and coffee.

Masterchef Goes Large. I've heard about it: the British elimination show with expat Aussie John Torode. It's punchy, fun, but not as over the top as the Americans. Thank God.

Heat in the Kitchen is something I'd been meaning to watch again anyway: Sydney chefs and Sydney restaurant critics fight it out in the great battle for *Good Food Guide* hats. I can relate.

Time for a spot of convalescent lunch—pasta and parmesan— as *Market Kitchen* mixes cooking and produce stories with food writer Matthew Fort and Tom Parker Bowles (yes, her son) looking about as jolly hockey sticks as you'd imagine.

Tamasin's *Great British Classics* has Daniel Day-Lewis' earnest little sister behaving a bit like Hugh Fearnley-Whittingstall without the sense of humour. If food and cooking's fun for our Tam, she hides it well.

Next up (with a little slumber en route) is our old mate Neil Perry with *Food Source*, which must be at least four years old.

There's a lot more grey in the ponytail these days. Good show then, good show now.

French Leave: John Burton Race's canal change to southern France. With a camera crew along for the ride. No wonder his family life's a mess.

More of the Gap man. He's still good. I still hate him.

And then the avuncular fish man and part-time Australian Rick Stein—from a few years back—making another show about Padstow. He owns Padstow, by the way. Ming Tsai (*Simply Ming*) demonstrates his appalling dress sense and ability to put at least one viewer to sleep almost immediately. I wake to *Food Fight* (having slept through Huey): it's high-five and yee-hahs as a couple of amateur marathon runners (men) cook off against a couple of bookish Ivy League types (women). More corn please.

Back to Australia for the straightforward but not unpleasant *Good Chef, Bad Chef* followed by *Heaven's Kitchen Cookbook*, an unashamed pitch to those of us vulnerable to the possibly non-existent mythical charms of a bucolic English idyll, to wit, host Mike Robinson's country village pub. Fantastic.

And Jamie; he had to come. It's no mistake the guy is prime time, but will we be watching re-runs of a 25-year-old Oliver when the guy's expecting his first grandchild?

Another snooze during *Chef at Home*. And dinner—more pasta and parmesan (with eggs)—in front of the *River Cottage* with the aforementioned Fearnley-Whittingstall. Is this the best series of food series ever?

Market Chef again … hey, I saw this at breakfast. Another episode of *Masterchef Goes Large*. And another of *Heat in the Kitchen*. We shuffle from Australia to the UK via the US, more or less constantly.

Rachel Allen (*Rachel's Favourite Food at Home*) is apparently famous. Why? She cooks baked potatoes. She's followed by a couple of forgettable Sloane rangers wasting an entire half-hour on choc-olate on *Chocolate Covered*. The programming seems to get lamer as the night gets older. It's not helping the mood or health.

But then it all comes good at 9.30pm when Peta Mathias' humble but informative *Taste Takes Off* explores the back streets of Hanoi. At 10pm, after a challenging day doing exactly nothing, I drag myself off the couch and into bed. I'm feeling a bit better. It's been an informative day.

Once upon a time you sought out the rare food program on television and chewed it up; now you can watch them 24 hours, seven days a week. What a concept. How sick would I need to be for that?

GRAEME BLUNDELL

Rude food

You can imagine Jamie Oliver saying of fellow television culinary master Gordon Ramsay, "Gordon ain't just a scrotum-faced sack of testosterone; he's got 10 Michelin stars, for Christ's sake." Chef ("It's my [expletive deleted] kitchen") Ramsay hates being labelled a celebrity chef and has little interest in seeing his "scrawny, crinkly, wrinkled face like the map of Wales coming out" on the screen.

But he is seemingly omnipresent, greatly (expletive deleted) talented, and back for the third series of the globally successful *The F Word*.

TV chefs are defining the meaning of cooking in this celebrity age. As Nigella Lawson once said, "cooking is the new rock'n'roll", presumably following hairdressing, reality TV, knitting, spelling bees, India and decorating.

The culinary Susan Sontag, who can so eruditely mention Marcel Proust in the same breath as praline, may be stretching it, but there's no doubt that cooking is losing its attachment to a living culture and becoming a new form of global entertainment.

Before Lawson, no one had ever so softly name-dropped ingredients as though they were designer labels. Food is increasingly part of the madness of popular culture, tied up with anxiety, guilt and fear. And in Ramsay's case, sex, as every show features the one-time professional soccer player topless.

Cooking shows, once considered a daytime format, conventionally gendered as feminine, are now a staple of mainstream, terrestrial programming, many of them fronted by hyperactive, testosterone-driven men such as Ramsay.

Their high-energy shows are a central part of the hybridisation of formats that characterises contemporary TV, often incorporating other styles of programming such as the travel show, game show and fly-on-the-wall documentary. Ramsay's brazen TV style looks like a foodie version of Jerry Bruckheimer's cop show aesthetic. *The F Word* is all explosive angles, extreme close-ups and rapid-fire editing. There is a mental acuteness at work, sophisticated, contrived, attention-grabbing.

In *The F Word* he has created a new TV genre, the foodie-friendly action-adventure, an MTV-paced foodie joy-ride. Every activity Ramsay engages in is sexy, glossy, high-camp fun.

He enters the first show in the new series like a parody of Marlon Brando before he started eating, prowling through the restaurant set, slamming down the bloody carcass of a deer and shouting, "There's dinner!"

Ramsay has become a kind of actor alive with resonance for his audience. He's almost Shakespearean in his delight in the big moment, his hysterical profanity and in his liking for live animals turned into carpaccio before our eyes.

He has constructed a big-top culinary circuit in which he revels, his passion for his food relentlessly under the spotlight. His series is a hybrid of cooking demonstration, TV food journalism, celebrity chat show, strident sitcom, and a reality-style behind-the-scenes look at the way great kitchens work.

There are also the mischievous stunts that bring the swearing, swaggering chef into controversial contact with guns, horsemeat, breast milk and the new superfood, blood.

In this episode, he treks off to Norway, diving through ice in a bulky dry suit in search of the monster king crab, the world's largest crustacean. "My balls feel like two (expletive deleted) ice cubes," he yells at the camera. (I think I had counted 43 uses of the f-word by this point. Ramsay leaves the profane *Deadwood* well behind in the swearing stakes.) When he's not out hunting and shooting or butchering hard-to-find things to eat, Ramsay's in the glamorous F Word restaurant with amateur brigades of wannabes trying to prove they have the skills and character to deliver under the pressure of a professional restaurant service.

And Ramsay is on a mission to find a talented female chef who can fill the shoes of legendary TV cook Fanny Cradock, as part of his "Get women back in the kitchen" campaign. Of course, it's called Find Me a Fanny.

Celebrity guest Dawn French can't help herself. "Interested in my fanny?" she asks, licking those lascivious lips. The pulchritudinous *Vicar of Dibley* actor seems to be a hit with the randy restaurateur, who can't stop snogging her.

You can't imagine the scholarly molecular gastronomist Heston Blumenthal copping a feel in *In Search of Perfection*; his show is more witty chemistry lesson than in-your-face cookery program. Blumenthal's Berkshire restaurant, The Fat Duck, was named world's best several years ago by a panel of international pundits and owns three Michelin stars. It is famous for its egg-and-bacon ice cream, tobacco chocolates and sardine-on-toast sorbet.

In his eight-part series, the stocky, oddly groovy Blumenthal, his cool obsessiveness totally captivating, focuses on some of Britain's classic dishes, from fish and chips to roast beef. This week, bangers and mash and treacle tart get the Blumenthal treatment. Dressed in white coat and safety goggles, he scientifically dismantles the traditional recipes with liquid nitrogen and thermally kinetic dry ice.

Like a mad scientist from a Jules Verne story, Blumenthal seeks to create the ultimate taste sensation in his purpose-built laboratory-style kitchen, using his famous pressure cookers, vacuum cleaners and gas chromatographs. He employs innovative ways to film the cooking process, too, with infrared, ultraviolet, heat sensitive micro-cams and graphics that illustrate molecular animation.

Blumenthal introduces us to food growers across the globe, as well as like-minded passionate researchers, making this a culinary version of Michael Palin's *Around the World in 80 Days*.

The abundance of TV chefs, especially one as ardently scientific as Blumenthal, probably confuses as much as it assists anyone at home trying to learn the subtleties of cooking. But the rest of us can drool over the populist, telegenic foodie flirts on the screen, soaking up their subliminal message about money, self-esteem and an elusively elegant lifestyle.

In their very different ways, Ramsay and Blumenthal have turned TV food into a new form of spectator sport, fascinating, sometimes frightening and always deeply humbling for anyone who thinks they know anything about cooking.

Contributors

Phillip Adams is Australia's most ancient newspaper columnist—fifty years and counting—and the ABC's most biased broadcaster. Although he has published twenty collections of jokes—and despite being described by Gough Whitlam as "Australia's greatest humourist"—he despises all forms of levity. He gets particularly angry when people describe his film *The Adventures of Barry McKenzie* as a comedy. Both that film and this column were "deadly serious".

David Astle has written two novels, a true-crime book plus a trivia-travel guide to Australia—and his publishers wish he'd settle for a single genre. "Oxtales", a short story, won the James Joyce Suspended Sentence in 2001, while his short plays have been performed in Sydney and Melbourne. He reviews books for Radio National, teaches journalism at RMIT and is also an incurable maker of cryptic crosswords.

Graeme Blundell is an actor, director, producer and writer who has been associated with many pivotal moments in Australian theatre, film and television. Now the national TV critic for *The Australian*, his autobiography, *The Naked Truth*, has just been published. He lives on the NSW coast with writer Susan Kurosawa.

The Chaser team has created the ABC TV series *The Election Chaser*, *CNNNN*, *The Chaser Decides* and *The Chaser's War on Everything*. Since founding the widely acclaimed but mostly unread newspaper *The Chaser* in 1999, the team has produced comedy in all major media, including TV, radio, books and Christmas cracker jokes. *The Chaser* is now a satirical media empire which rivals Rupert Murdoch's News Corp in all fields except power, influence, popularity and profitability.

Barry Cohen was a federal MP from 1969 until 1990, including Minister for Home Affairs and Environment from 1983 to 1984, Minister for Arts, Heritage and Environment from 1984 to 1987 and the Minister Assisting the Prime Minister for the Bicentennial. He is the author of several books and a regular contributor to some of Australia's leading magazines and newspapers including *The Australian*.

Kaz Cooke is a columnist and author. Her website is www.kaz .cooke.com

Ian Cuthbertson began his liquorice allsorts freelance writing career in the 1980s. He was engaged by *The Australian* as a contributor in late 1996, and his adoption was made formal following a full-time job offer in 2002. He builds his own computers, runs a project music studio and is currently *The Australian*'s television and DVD editor.

Mark Dapin is a writer for *Good Weekend Magazine* in *The Sydney Morning Herald* and *The Age*. His latest book is *Strange Country*, the story of his travels around Australia. In another life, he was editor-in-chief of *Ralph Magazine*.

Catherine Deveny is a serial pest and professional pain in the arse. She writes columns for the big paper with the big words despite being dyslexic and half-cocked.

Frank Devine has been editor of the *New York Post*, the *Chicago Sun Times* and *The Australian*. He now lives in Sydney and writes regularly for *The Australian*.

Alexander Downer was Australia's Foreign Affairs Minister for twelve years. He was instrumental in delivering independence in East Timor and played a pivotal role in Australia's response to the Middle East conflicts. He has been an active participant and diplomatic force on global issues of human rights, climate change and natural disasters. He is now a United Nations Special Envoy for Cyprus.

Larissa Dubecki is a news reporter for *The Age*. She was the editor of *The Age*'s weekly entertainment lift-out *EG* until August 2006, and currently writes on topics relating to entertainment and popular culture, including reviewing television for the *Green Guide* and restaurants for the *Good Food Guide* and *Cheap Eats Guide*.

Suzanne Edgar, as a member of Seven Writers, wrote *Canberra Tales*, and her short stories were published as *Counting Backwards*. Her poetry collection, *The Painted Lady*, was short-listed for the ACT's Best Book of the Year and for the 2007 ACT Writing and Publishing awards.

Charles Firth is a leading think-piece writer, boasting more than 55 000 opinions about the world, all of them less than one sentence long. He delivered the keynote at the 2008 World Cynicism Symposium in San Diego, where he expressed thirty-seven controversial opinions in under twenty seconds, setting a new world record.

Germaine Greer was born in Melbourne and educated in Australia and at Cambridge University. Her first book, *The Female Eunuch*, remains one of the most influential texts of the feminist movement. Germaine has had a distinguished academic career in Britain and the US, and makes regular appearances in print and other media as a broadcaster, journalist, columnist and reviewer. Since 1988 she has been director (and financier) of Stump Cross Books, a publishing house specialising in lesser known works by early women writers.

Gideon Haigh is vice-president and chairman of selectors at South Yarra Cricket Club.

Marieke Hardy is a writer, radio broadcaster, hedonist and raconteur. After an ill-advised early career as a child actress she carried on polluting Australian television airwaves via her work as a screenwriter and producer. She is very sorry about any damage caused to your carpets.

Matthew Hardy is a Melbourne-based comedian who was the first Aussie to cement himself full-time on the UK live circuit, spending eight years there in the 1990s. He is the author of the bestselling book *Saturday Afternoon Fever*, and his television credits include *The Big Schmooze* and *The Fat*. Matthew was also a part of the BAFTA-winning writing team for *The Sketch Show* on ITV in the UK, and subsequently wrote for Kelsey Grammer's sketch series on Fox in the US.

Wendy Harmer hosted *The Big Gig* on ABC TV and Sydney's highest rating FM radio breakfast show for eleven years. She has written seven books for adults and ten for children, and she wrote, produced and presented the documentary series *Stuff* for ABC TV. Wendy is currently writing and producing an animated television series based on her *Pearlie* books, and her third novel for adults.

Barry Humphries is a multi-talented actor, artist and author. As an actor, he has invented many satiric Australian characters, but his most famous creations are Dame Edna Everage, Barry (Bazza)

McKenzie and Sir Les Paterson. Edna, Bazza and Les between them have made several sound recordings, written books and appeared in films and on television and have been the subject of exhibitions. Since the 1960s Humphries' career has alternated between England, Australia and the US. He was given an Order of Australia in 1982.

Clive James is the author of more than thirty books. As well as his four volumes of autobiography, he has published novels and collections of literary and television criticism, essays, travel writing and verse. As a television performer he has appeared regularly for both the BBC and ITV. In 1992 he was made a Member of the Order of Australia and in 2003 he was awarded the Philip Hodgins Memorial Medal for Literature.

Danny Katz is a columnist for *The Age* and *The Sydney Morning Herald*. He is the "Modern Guru" in the *Good Weekend Magazine*. He is the author of several books including *Spid the Dummy, Dork Geek Jew* and the *Little Lunch* series for kids. Danny is originally from Canada, but came to Australia at a young age because he was allergic to maple syrup.

Malcolm Knox is the author of ten books, most recently *On Obsession*. His works of fiction and non-fiction have won several awards and have been published around the world. A journalist since 1994 for *The Sydney Morning Herald*, he has won two Walkley awards.

Peter Lalor is a senior sports writer with *The Australian* and has written a number of books including *Blood Stain*, winner of the 2004 Ned Kelly Award for True Crime Writing. He lives with his wife, two children and a brown dog in Sydney, but learned about darkness in 1980s Melbourne.

John Lethlean is fortunate enough to write about the subjects he loves—food and restaurants—for a living, mostly for titles associated with *The Age*. When he's not being a proper critic, he has a bit of fun with a food-related column in the Saturday *Age*, where the pieces in this collection were first published.

Mungo MacCallum has been writing and broadcasting irreverently about politics for more than forty years. His work has appeared in most major Australian and some overseas publications. He is the author of seven books, the most recent being *Poll Dancing: The Story of the 2007 Election.*

Shane Maloney is the editor of *Speleology Today*, the world's biggest selling glow-in-the-dark monthly magazine. He is better known as the author of the Murray Whelan series of comic thrillers.

Shaun Micallef is a writer, comedian actor, TV producer and professional tennis player. He is married and has three children.

Paul Mitchell's latest books are a collection of short stories titled *Dodging the Bull*, and a poetry collection, *Awake Despite the Hour*, both published in 2007. He'd like to say something else but is too busy answering his email.

Les Murray is a fair poet but a poor cook at best. He lives in the Australian bush.

Olga Pavlinova Olenich was born in Australia of Russian parentage. She is a Melbourne-based writer whose stories, articles and poetry are widely published in Australia and overseas. She has one son, who is a musician.

Rod Quantock is one of the reasons that Melbourne is the live comedy capital of Australia. For forty years he has remained a contemporary stand-up comedian, evolving and staying at the forefront of the craft. That he continues to build new, younger audiences is testament to possibly the most impressive career in Australian comedy.

Guy Rundle is currently the US correspondent for *Crikey*. He was co-editor of *Arena Magazine* between 1992 and 2006 and is a frequent contributor to a wide range of Australian publications, and the writer of a number of hit stage shows with the satirist Max Gillies.

Roy Slaven, together with HG Nelson, has presented *This Sporting Life* on Triple J for more than twenty years.

Garry Williams is the *Sunday Herald Sun*'s TV guide editor. A journalist for more than twenty-five years, his main claim to fame is as a former *TV Week* editor, although he is happy to report that he has upset enough people to never again be invited to the Logie Awards.

Tony Wilson is an author who has written one novel (*Players*), a World Cup fan's memoir (*Australia United*) and four picture books for children. In 2006 he was a *Sydney Morning Herald* Young Australian Novelist of the Year. He has also worked in radio and television. Tony's website is www.tonywilson.com.au

Julia Zemiro is best known as host of AFI Award–winning SBS TV show *RocKwiz*. Her TV credits include *Thank God You're Here* and *What a Year*, co-hosting with Bert Newton, and her theatre roles include *Love Song* and *Eurobeat—The Eurovision Musical*. Julia is the co-host of the nationally syndicated radio show *The Jonathan Coleman Experience*.

Acknowledgements

Phillip Adams, "My 2UE producer noticed a tendency for me to nod off during interviews. In my own defence, they lined up some boring farts", *The Australian Weekend Magazine*, 4 August 2007.

David Astle, "I came, I buzzed, I lost". The piece in this collection is an updated version of an article originally published in *Sunday Life* magazine in March 2002.

Graeme Blundell, "Rude food", *The Weekend Australian*, *Review* supplement, 22 September 2007.

Barry Cohen, "Modern telecoms run rings around me", *The Australian*, 14 April 2008.

Kaz Cooke, "Phwoarr, check out the policies on Julia Gillard", *The Age*, 14 March 2006. This article was originally published in *The Age* under the headline "Julia's not got what it takes? Balls!"

—— "Planet Earth: Beware of the chimps", *The Canberra Times*, 13 February 2007, reproduced at <www.kazcooke.com.au/kazcooke/columns/07feb13.html>.

Ian Cuthbertson, "You just know it will be deliciously messy", *The Weekend Australian*, *Review* supplement, 19 April 2008.

The piece in this collection is an edited extract of an article originally published in *The Australian*.

Mark Dapin, "Adventures in LA-Land", *The Age Good Weekend Magazine*, 25–27 April 2008. Mark Dapin would like to thank Judith Whelan at *Good Weekend* for sending him to LA to cover an event that didn't happen.

Catherine Deveny, "Listen up, you selfish and ignorant people. Stop driving 4WDs", *The Age*, 28 March 2007.

Frank Devine, "All is not lost when you can see success in anything", *The Australian*, 7 December 2007.

—— "It's a loathe-hate relationship, but at least I own a slice", *The Australian*, 21 December 2007.

Alexander Downer, "The satire we had to have: Keating", *The Advertiser*, 29 March 2008.

Larissa Dubecki, "Madonna's latest offering leaves listener pondering: Just because she can, does it mean she should?", *The Age*, 25–26 April 2008.

Suzanne Edgar, "Song of the crestfallen pigeon", *Quadrant*, vol. LI, no. 6, June 2007.

Dame Edna Everage, "My loyal subjects and possums! A seasonal message from President Edna", *The Bulletin*, vol. 125, no. 51, 18 December 2007.

Charles Firth, "A hookworm's-eye view of the world around us", *The Sydney Morning Herald*, 25 October 2007.

—— "Lies, damned lies", *The Monthly*, May 2008.

Germaine Greer, "So Ian McKellen drops his trousers to play King Lear. That sums up the RSC's whole approach", *The Guardian*, 7 May 2007.

—— "Who cares if she can't sing and can't dance? Posh Spice is the Damien Hirst of dress-wearing", *The Guardian*, 19 May 2008.

Gideon Haigh, "Packed it in: The demise of the *Bulletin*", *The Monthly*, March 2008.

Andrew Hansen, Dominic Knight, Chas Licciardello, Julian Morrow and Craig Reucassel, "*The Chaser*'s Logies", *The Age*, 1 May 2008.

Marieke Hardy, "A time to repent: *Big Brother*'s over", *The Age*, *Green Guide* supplement, 9 August 2007.

—— "Lashings of lust curved up by Nigella", *The Age*, *Green Guide* supplement, 24 January 2008.

—— "Er, thanks for your support. No, don't call us, we'll call you", *The Age*, 5 June 2008.

Matthew Hardy, "Pump more beer, iron out muscle", *Herald Sun*, 5 January 2008.

Wendy Harmer, "Torn between satay skewers and children as an endangered species", *The Sydney Morning Herald*, 26 January 2007.

Clive James, "On climate change", *A Point of View*, radio broadcast, BBC Radio 4, 2 and 4 February 2007, transcript viewed August 2008. Reprinted by permission of United Agents on behalf of Clive James.

—— "The perfectly bad sentence", *The Monthly*, February 2008. Reprinted by permission of United Agents on behalf of Clive James.

Danny Katz, "Love is never saying sorry ... so there", *The Age*, 14 February 2008.

Malcolm Knox, "Corporatising culture: Who holds the past in common trust?", *The Monthly*, February 2007.

Peter Lalor, "Fashion pinkoes are the fifth columnists of masculinity", *The Australian*, 17 August 2007.

John Lethlean, "Telly tubbies", *The Age*, 9 June 2007. John Lethlean would like to acknowledge Jonathan Green and Sally Heath, the first a former editor of *A2* at *The Age* and the latter, the current wearer of that hat.

—— "Silence of the lamb", *The Age*, 1 December 2007. John Lethlean would like to acknowledge Jonathan Green and Sally

Heath, the first a former editor of *A2* at *The Age* and the latter, the current wearer of that hat.

Mungo MacCallum, "The pollies went a little crackers", *The Bulletin*, vol. 125, no. 51, 18 December 2007.

Shane Maloney, "In from a busy day at Barwon jail, Carl asks for a fair go", *The Age*, 28 April 2007.

—— "Cook's tour: Peter Cook", *The Bulletin*, vol. 125, no. 51, 18 December 2007.

Shaun Micallef, "My father sat on Winston Churchill", *The Age*, 29 December 2006.

Paul Mitchell, "Contact", *Overland*, vol. 184, Spring 2006.

Les Murray, "Fame", *Quadrant*, vol. LI, no. 4, April 2007.

Olga Pavlinova Olenich, "Teacherwoman", *Overland*, vol. 189, Summer 2007.

Rod Quantock, "Group giggles groovy again", *The Age*, 15 April 2006.

Guy Rundle, "The right wing", *The Sunday Age*, 8 July 2007.

—— "Don't worry, just testing", *The Sunday Age*, 30 December 2007.

Roy Slaven, "Seven modern wonders indeed? I think not", *The Age*, 11 July 2007.

Steve Vizard, "The Library hotel, Thailand, and other hip hotels". This article was written for this collection.

Garry Williams, Interview with Ja'mie King, *Sunday Herald Sun*, 21 October 2007. The piece in this collection was taken from a longer article titled "Ja'mie's frocky horror".

Tony Wilson, "Having a ball: How we finally fell in love with the world game", *The Age Melbourne Magazine*, November 2007. The piece in this collection is an extended version of an article originally published in *The Age*.

Julia Zemiro, "Idle hands make for short nails", *Herald Sun*, 1 September 2007.